THE DEEP CHANGE
FIELD GUIDE

THE DEEP CHANGE FIELD GUIDE

A PERSONAL COURSE TO DISCOVERING THE LEADER WITHIN

Robert E. Quinn

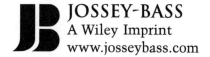

JOSSEY-BASS
A Wiley Imprint
www.josseybass.com

Published by Jossey-Bass
A Wiley Imprint
One Montgomery Street, Suite 1200, San Francisco, CA 94104-4594—www.josseybass.com

Jossey-Bass books and products are available through most bookstores. To contact Jossey-Bass directly call our Customer Care Department within the U.S. at 800-956-7739, outside the U.S. at 317-572-3986, or fax 317-572-4002.

Wiley publishes in a variety of print and electronic formats and by print-on-demand. Some material included with standard print versions of this book may not be included in e-books or in print-on-demand. If this book refers to media such as a CD or DVD that is not included in the version you purchased, you may download this material at http://booksupport.wiley.com. For more information about Wiley products, visit www.wiley.com.

Library of Congress Cataloging-in-Publication Data

Quinn, Robert E.
   The deep change field guide : a personal course to discovering the leader within / Robert E. Quinn. – First edition.
      pages cm. – (The Jossey-Bass Business & Management Series)
   Includes bibliographical references and index.
   ISBN 978-0-470-90216-5 (pbk.), 978-1-118-22114-3 (ebk), 978-1-118-23503-4 (ebk), 978-1-118-25959-7 (ebk)
  1.   Organizational change—Management. 2.   Leadership.   I. Title.
   HD58.8.Q564 2012
   658.4'092—dc23

                        2011052640

Printed in the United States of America

FIRST EDITION
PB Printing 10 9 8 7 6 5 4 3 2 1

The Jossey-Bass Business & Management Series

To Roger W. Thomas

CONTENTS

PREFACE

The Deep Change Field Guide, based on my book *Deep Change,* is about finding ways to negotiate our constantly changing world. It is about the move from being reactive to being proactive. It is about growing when it is tempting to surrender. Its purpose is to help you empower yourself and the communities in which you operate.

I have been writing about change for a long time. *Deep Change* was published in 1996. It was based on the simple notion that as individuals and organizations we must adapt or die. When we are faced with novel challenges, we almost always feel that it would be easier to simply keep doing what we did before. The choice to stay in our comfort zones represents the path of least resistance. The choice to change is far more difficult.

Deep Change was written to help us choose change and move forward. It described how people who committed to change found themselves transformed by that commitment. They became change agents as the energy they found in themselves became contagious. They gained the power to help those around them transform themselves and to revitalize their relationship, group, or organization. This is the essence of deep change.

In *Change the World* (2000), I explained that great change leaders shared a number of characteristics. They were deeply committed to their cause, developed a vision of what they wanted the world to be like, and devoted themselves to finding ways to bring change about. They cared little about what other people thought of them, but they cared deeply about the people around them. Above all, they wanted to help the people around them break out of the slow death process—they wanted to change the world by teaching others how to change. A significant element of the process was the teachers' commitment to continually changing themselves.

As I read stories sent to me by the many people who read my books, I saw many connections to principles I had articulated. I then wrote *Building the Bridge As You Walk On It* (2004). In that book, I articulated a new concept called the *fundamental state of leadership*, which emphasized how leadership does not depend on position. Instead, leadership comes from influence. As we react to our ever-changing context, the nature and effectiveness of our influence vary continually. By taking charge of our own psychological state, we can alter our influence and the quality of our experience. We can choose to enter the fundamental state of leadership.

Finally, in *Lift: Becoming a Positive Force in Any Situation* (2009), my son Ryan and I integrated the fundamental state of leadership with the science of positive psychology and positive organizational scholarship. We demonstrated the academic basis for the concept and provided tools for application.

That brings us to the present volume. The goal of *The Deep Change Field Guide* is to help you understand and apply the deep change concept in your life. The field guide first presents the essence of the material in *Deep Change* and then adds a sprinkling of content from *Change the World* and *Building the Bridge As You Walk On It*, while interspersing questions and activities to help you learn.

As you go through the field guide, you may be surprised to learn that you already possess the tools you need. Because our culture places great emphasis on hierarchy and expertise, we assume that education is a process in which experts instill knowledge based on past experiences into passive recipients. This guide follows a different model. It invites you to reflect on the experiences of others, actively apply that knowledge to your own life, and seek inside yourself the tools of personal change. As you transform yourself through this process, you will learn how to help others find within themselves the capacity to change. By opening yourself to new learning and questioning your assumptions, you will become a transformational leader.

I invite you now to begin a journey that will change your life.

* * * * *

Many people have worked hard to make this book possible. I would like to particularly thank three. Kathe Sweeney constantly pushed and inspired. She was a great leader. Seth Soderborg was instrumental in managing every phase of moving the book forward. He was brilliant and disciplined. Janis Chan was a marvelous developmental editor who improved everything. My thanks go to each one.

Robert E. Quinn

ABOUT THIS FIELD GUIDE

The Deep Change Field Guide is a self-teaching course that will help you embark on a journey of personal transformation. Each chapter includes clear explanations of the key concepts of deep change with stories to illustrate them, reflection questions to help you think about the concepts and apply them to your own life, and activities to help you pull together what you have learned and focus on your insights.

THINK ABOUT IT

As you read each chapter, you will find a number of questions that are designed to help you reflect on specific concepts in terms of yourself and your organization.

PERSONAL REFLECTION AND APPLICATION

Each chapter ends with several activities. Each one is designed to help you internalize the notions in the book. We encourage you to engage them.

Reflect

The first activity at the end of the chapter asks you to quickly write down the points, concepts, or ideas that stand out for you the most while they are fresh in your mind.

Watch a Film

The next end-of-chapter activity is a film assignment. It is perhaps the most important activity of all, and we strongly encourage you to make it a part of your experience. The films are readily available on DVD or through online or mail-order services such as Netflix. They have been selected to help you discover the ways in which transformative experiences lead people to change themselves and help others achieve deep change. The questions are designed to help you think about how the leaders in the films exemplify these concepts and then apply that learning to your own situation. Here's a list of the films you will watch:

Chapter 1—*Norma Rae*
Chapter 2—*Moneyball*
Chapter 3—*The King's Speech*
Chapter 4—*The Devil Wears Prada*
Chapter 5—*Remember the Titans*
Chapter 6—*Stand and Deliver*
Chapter 7—*Gandhi*
Chapter 8—*Dead Poets Society*

Make a Journal Entry

Keeping a leadership journal is an excellent way to expand and continue your learning. This activity asks you to select statements from the chapter that resonate with you and then reflect on life experiences you relate to those concepts.

Write a Memo

Writing a memo to someone you know (whether or not you actually send it) about what you learned in the chapter helps you pull together your insights from the Think About It questions, the quick reflection, the film, and the journal activity to focus on the essence of what you learned.

Apply the Learning

The best way to learn something is to do it. The last activity in each chapter asks you to select some actions you will take to begin and continue your journey toward mastery of the deep change process.

PUT THE LEARNING TO WORK

The final chapter of the book will help you pull together what you have learned from this field guide about the process of deep change and decide how you will use that learning.

GETTING THE MOST FROM THIS COURSE

Everyone learns differently. You might want to read the field guide quickly, then go back to read through each chapter one at a time, answering the questions and doing the activities. Or, you might want to take one chapter, or even one section of a chapter, at a time, so you can assimilate the concepts at your preferred pace. Take the course in whatever way works best for you.

Here are a few suggestions to help you get the most value from the learning process.

- Take enough time to think about the questions and do the activities. There are no right or wrong answers to the questions, and no right or wrong ways to do the activities. By being thoughtful and allowing yourself enough time, you will greatly increase the value of the course.
- Write down your responses to the questions. It doesn't matter whether you write in the book itself or make notes on your computer: the act of writing helps you understand the concepts and retain your insights. Your written notes also will provide a reference you can return to later.
- Although the films are very engaging, you will learn less if you think of them as entertainment. Instead, think of them as case studies that provide deep lessons on transformational leadership. Since transformation is a difficult concept for

the left brain to grasp, watching the videos and engaging your right brain will make a big difference in your learning experience.

Before watching a film, read the accompanying discussion questions. While you are watching the people in the film face a challenge, put yourself in their shoes and ask what you would do. Pause the film as needed to note your observations.

When you have finished watching, write down your answers to the questions. If any of your colleagues are also taking this course, it's a good idea to watch the films and discuss the questions together.

THE DEEP CHANGE
FIELD GUIDE

CHAPTER ONE

AN INVITATION TO CHANGE

IN THIS CHAPTER

- Change attempts often fail because of the assumptions we make.
- We often find ourselves in situations that require us to adapt but choose to distort reality and deny what the world is telling us.
- To be excellent, we have to be at the edge, a place of uncertainty and learning.
- When we are committed to a higher purpose, we move forward through the fear of conflict, and as we do, we learn and we see in new ways.

I recently received a phone call from an information technology executive whose team had spent months designing a technical change that was about to be launched across the corporation. Other senior people had consistently advised him to talk to someone who "understands change in terms of people and culture" before rolling out the change. So he asked me to come in and speak to his team about how to implement the change process. He also mentioned that his people were not very interested in hearing about the role of culture in their change effort and could see little value in such a visit.

This executive was a very educated and experienced man. Yet he was about to launch a companywide change without having considered the role of culture in the change process. Such ignorance is unimaginable—it's the equivalent of learning that your brain surgeon is ignorant of the organ known as the heart. Yet such ignorance is also very widespread; it often seems as though ignorance about the importance of organizational culture is an epidemic. I hold the radical belief that many people do not know how to lead change, including people who think they already have.

Think About It

- Why did this executive spend months planning a change without considering his company's culture? Where was he focusing his attention?

  _____

  _____

  _____

- Have you ever been involved in leading an organizational change effort? What was the primary focus—on the mechanical processes or the needs for human learning involved in the change? What was the result? Looking back, what do you think you should have done differently?

  _____

  _____

  _____

- How might you plan a change effort to take culture into account? What would you do to be credible when you asked others to change their behavior?

  _____

  _____

  _____

THE WESTERN WAY

Jeff Liker is perhaps the world's leading outside expert on how work is done at Toyota. When I spoke with him not long ago, he explained that, despite the glitches that came to light in 2010, Toyota had been so successful that thousands of companies have attempted to implement the Toyota concept of lean manufacturing. *Lean* is a philosophy of excellence that puts a heavy emphasis on the customer and the value chain. Implementing this concept, managers work to eliminate waste through a process of continuous improvement.

But Jeff pointed out that only 2 percent of companies that have implemented lean have achieved the anticipated results, and many of those ultimately experienced disappointment. These failures represent billions of dollars in lost value.

Why have the results been so miserable? At Toyota they understand something about change that few Western companies understand. Western companies operate with a checklist mentality. An expert comes up with the "correct" way to do something, builds a plan, trains the people, and audits the change progress. The great thing about this approach is that it is fast and efficient. The bad thing is that it seldom works. Worse, we often fail to see that it does not work.

THE CHECKLIST MENTALITY

As Jeff was talking, I recalled a quality evaluation program called Q1 that Ford introduced in the 1980s to stimulate deep change. To obtain the Q1 award, a plant had to pass an examination given by a group of hard-nosed outside evaluators. Leaders from successful plants were often invited to share their strategies with other groups.

At the time, my colleagues and I at the University of Michigan were running a professional development program for three thousand middle managers at Ford. Sometimes, we invited Q1 award winners to give presentations.

These presenters would usually recount the plant's general history, describe their results from the Q1 effort, and explain what had been done to obtain the results. The discussion would then turn to the issue of greatest interest for the audience: How could another plant achieve similar results?

At this point, the presenter would usually talk about things like the need for "everyone" to learn. He or she might talk of equality, participation, risk-taking, continual experiments, authentic communication, mutual learning, the transformation of assumptions, and the joint implementation of new ideas. (The presenter was actually talking about the subject of this book: leading deep change.) These discussions made the managers uneasy. After a few minutes, someone would invariably say, "Give me specifics. What do I need to do and when?"

I asked one presenter about this pattern. He explained, "They just don't understand. They want a checklist, but this is not about checklists. This is about figuring out where you are and where you need to go and then launching an effort to get there. It's about learning together. The key to becoming a Q1 plant is finding the unique strategy for your plant. Once you find it, you have to start looking for the next one, the one that will be right for tomorrow. There are no recipes." Few people want to hear that last sentence. It suggests that we need to do a kind of work that no one wants to do: the work of deep change.

Thirty years later, we are having the same conversations. The reason why today's executives look at Toyota's success, invest heavily in change, and then fail miserably is because successful implementation of a successful model is not about copying some existing technology. Rather, it is about changing culture, which means changing the way people have thought and acted for years. It is about learning how to learn together and create excellence in real time.

Leading deep change is never easy. But *why* is it so hard to understand and lead deep change?

Think About It

- Have you ever been part of a change effort in which your organization tried to import processes that others had used successfully? What were the results? What were some of the reasons for those results? Why might something that worked in one organization not work in another?

  _____

  _____

  _____

- When you look to examples of success to guide your own actions, do you prefer examples that provide concrete steps, tell you what to do and when to do it? What if an example did not provide concrete how-to steps? Could you use it? How?

  _____

  _____

  _____

CHALLENGE YOUR NORMAL ASSUMPTIONS

The process of leading deep change violates the assumptions that normally guide our interactions with others. Thus, simply telling people about that process will not show them why it works—the explanation just bounces off of their strongly held normal assumptions. Deep change begins with a state of mind. When I teach deep change, I no longer try to explain. Instead, I put people through experiences that cause them to challenge their own assumptions.

For example, I sometimes use a simple role-play to show that resistance to the ideas of deep change is not limited to corporate managers. Two volunteers play spouses who have just returned from their honeymoon. After breakfast, the "wife" leans back and lights up a cigarette. The "husband" is concerned about her smoking but has never raised the issue. He decides that he can no longer suppress his concern. I ask him to begin a conversation with his beloved. The objective is to get her to quit smoking.

The dynamics are predictable. The husband tells the wife that her smoking is a problem. She grows defensive and angry. He points out the scientific link between smoking and cancer. She rebuffs this argument. Then he suggests that their marriage may not survive if she continues to smoke. She usually agrees that the marriage might not survive. The intervention fails. This pattern is repeated nearly every time the simulation is run.

Think About It

- What happened during that role-play? Why does this kind of intervention nearly always fail?

  _____

  _____

  _____

- When was the last time you tried to get someone else to change, at work or in your personal life? Was the intervention successful? Why or why not?

  _____

  _____

  _____

- Think about a time when someone wanted you to make a change. How did the person talk to you about it? If he or she used rational arguments, how did that make you feel? Did those arguments convince you to change? Why or why not?

  _____

  _____

  _____

- If someone wanted you to make a change, how would you suggest they go about it? What kinds of things could they do or say to convince you to change?

  _____

  _____

  _____

That role-play is an example of a very common kind of interaction. One person defines the other as having a problem, thus taking on a higher role in an assumed hierarchical system. Person 1 communicates the problem and Person 2 resists. Person 1 now defines the other person (or people) *as* the problem, transforming him or her (or them) into an object that needs fixing. Person 1 takes the expert role and provides a rational argument for why Person 2 must change. He or she continues to resist. The first person shifts to intimidation. Person 2 becomes more defensive and, sometimes, more assertive. Person 1 might then turn to coercion. Like a criminal with a gun, he or she may get the desired behavior change, but change made this way is unlikely to last, and coercion fatally wounds relationships over the long term.

The attempt to "engineer" other people's behavior is one of the primary reasons why so many organizational change efforts fail. Most failed CEOs lose their jobs because they cannot get their employees to change in such a way as to deliver increased performance. Despite their enormous authority, their careful plans and strategies, they are unable to lead people through the process of change. They are trapped in our normal assumptions of hierarchy, control, linearity, expertise, achievement, and recognition.

COLLECTIVE LEARNING

When Jeff Liker talks about Toyota, he explains something he calls a *collective learning process* in which two or more people learn in real time as they move forward together. In this process, everyone learns from everyone else. The notion of authority fades into the background.

One of his favorite examples is the story of a manufacturing firm that hired a Toyota expert as a consultant to improve its processes.

After touring the manufacturing site, the consultant said, "You have three shifts with a total of 140 employees. I suggest that we reduce to two shifts with a total of ten people while maintaining the current level of productivity."

Naturally, the managers' first question was, "How?"

Please carefully note the consultant's answer: "I do not know."

A normal consultant would have given an answer even if he had to make it up. Consultants have a profound need to look like experts, a trait they share with the rest of us. We are afraid of what will happen if others find out we do not know all the answers.

The consultant added, "We will have to learn our way to our goal. I would like you to concentrate your efforts on eliminating the inventory backlog. In a few weeks, I will come back and see what you have learned."

The people in the manufacturing firm worked hard to eliminate the backlog. They met often, tried experiments, and listened to each other. In the process they learned to interact as equals. They generated a number of innovations and were excited to share them when the consultant returned. The consultant reinforced their efforts and then turned their attention to another part of the process. This pattern continued for two years. At the end of two years, the firm was down to two shifts and had reduced the workforce from 140 to 15.

This is a rather dramatic outcome. As they looked back on what happened, it was clear that they had a vision and they pursued it as a team in the process of collective learning. It had to be more than a linear process articulated ahead of time by an expert who then measured and controlled what happened. It had to include a change process based on adaptation. They tried things, worked together to evaluate the results, and then made adjustments and tried again. As they communicated with one another, their assumptions changed. Together, they learned the way to their goal: they built the bridge as they walked on it. It was a process of deep change.

Think About It

- Why are people often uncomfortable with a change process that involves setting a goal and deciding over time how to accomplish it, instead of following a checklist?

  _____

  _____

  _____

- Control over the collective learning process comes from trust. Have you ever been a part of an organization that was full of trust? How did that high level of trust change the way people interacted with each other?

  _____

  _____

  _____

- What are some things that people in organizations can do to increase trust so they can engage in a collective learning process?

  _____

  _____

  _____

TWO KINDS OF CHANGE: INCREMENTAL CHANGE AND DEEP CHANGE

Most of the changes we experience and lead can be classified as incremental changes. *Incremental change* is change based on past experiences. Our experiences become a series of assumptions that we make about cause and effect. We see change as a mechanical process, one that we can control. We think we know what adjustments must be made for the desired result to occur. Because we assume we are in control, we act upon others, directing them with a clear expectation of what the outcome will look like.

Deep change is a fundamentally different process because it requires people to develop new expectations. As people experience deep change, they move from their old assumptions to a new set of assumptions. They start to see, feel, and think differently. Soon, they behave differently. To get a child to put her bike away, for example, we can drag her outside and demand that she do it. This does not guarantee that the bike will be in the right place tomorrow night. We need her to see, feel, and think differently. When she does, we will no longer have to direct her. She will put her bike away because putting her bike away is a part of who she is.

In the deep change process, we surrender control as it is normally understood. It is tempting to say that we give up control. That is not quite so. It is more accurate to say that we shift to another kind of control. We join with others in relationships of trust. As we do so, we extend that trust to create collective intelligence and capacity. We must move forward, experimenting and paying attention to feedback in real time. We share with others everything we are learning, and they do the same.

As this collective learning process unfolds, we begin to accomplish things that we could never have accomplished alone. We discover that excellence is a form of deviance, that we can only be excellent if we are not doing what is normal. We must be at the edge of where we feel comfortable, because the place of uncertainty is a place of learning. Learning is the engine of deep change; as we put ourselves into uncertain places, our assumptions change and we grow. We increase our capacity best by being fully challenged. But challenge is not enough. For us to turn uncertainty into personal transformation, we must be supported and encouraged in the process of engagement and learning. This kind of growth makes us into more effective versions of ourselves, allowing us to become empowered individuals and empowering members of our community.

Deep change requires us to recognize that we are not experts with superior logic. Leaders of deep change are visionaries with a driving desire to enact their given vision. They are not acting upon people—they are acting with them. Assumptions of hierarchy become latent or dormant as people learn together in networks of equality.

Think About It

- Why is it possible to be excellent only when we are not doing what is normal?

  _____

  _____

  _____

- What kinds of things can we learn when we leave our comfort zones?

  _____

  _____

  _____

- Have you ever changed because of something you learned when you were dealing with uncertainty? What was the experience like?

  _____

  _____

  _____

BECOMING A TRANSFORMATIONAL LEADER: AN ANALOGY

In his book *The Man Who Listens to Horses* (1997), Monty Roberts tells how he discovered his potential. Monty grew up with a father who trained horses. Actually, his father "broke horses," using violent physical force.

Monty's father based his approach to horse training on assumptions of control. The objective was to subjugate the horse, break its spirit, and make it a slave to the rider's will. Seeing how the broken horses suffered, the young Monty vowed to find a better way.

On visits to Nevada as a youngster, Monty became fascinated with wild mustangs. He spent long hours observing these horses in the wilderness. He watched how they used their bodies to establish relationships, communicate, and shape behavior in the herd. He formulated hypotheses about what he was seeing. He began to recognize the hidden or deep organization of the herd.

Based on his reflection, Monty began experimenting with ways to use his eyes, hands, and body to communicate with the animals. Through trial and error, he was eventually able to communicate in the language of the herd. His goal was to build trust. Monty would adapt to the horse and the horse to Monty as each learned about the other. This would continue until the horse was willing to allow Monty to climb on and ride.

Monty eventually learned to train horses in a fraction of the time that it took his father and his father's colleagues. His process was not only faster, his horses were more dependable and more responsive. Monty began transforming animals that other trainers had given up on. He even trained wild mustangs to be gentle mounts, a feat that many trainers had considered impossible.

Monty became a master of change because of a disciplined self-change effort. He paid deep attention to how horses organize themselves, coming to know things that most people in his profession never learn. Through this process, he developed *adaptive confidence,* a belief that he could move forward into uncertain situations and learn what he needed to know as he needed it. Masters of deep change often have a universal theory of change; they tend to believe in their capacity to bring about transformation in nearly any situation.

A SECOND ANALOGY

What does becoming a master of horse training have to do with becoming a leader of deep change? There are vast differences between training horses and changing human systems. In examining any phenomenon it is natural to see differences. With more work, it is often possible to see deeper commonalities. When we learn to see commonality, we cross normal conceptual boundaries and we gain insights that open the door to new possibilities. If we are willing to learn from many different examples, we gain unusual new insights. We can see that Monty Roberts's careful reflection and willingness to try new methods is an example of the care and openness to learning that characterize transformational leaders in every human system.

Here is another example. Describing a master craftsman repairing a motorcycle, Robert Pirsig, author of *Zen and the Art of Motorcycle Maintenance* (1974), writes:

Look at a novice workman or a bad workman and compare his expression with that of a craftsman whose work you know is excellent and you'll see the difference. The craftsman isn't ever following a single line of instruction. He's making decisions as he goes along. For that reason he'll be absorbed and attentive to what he is doing even though he doesn't deliberately contrive this. His motions and the machine are in a kind of harmony. He isn't following any set of written instructions because the nature of the material at hand determines his thoughts and motions, which simultaneously change the nature of the material at hand. The material and his thoughts are changing together in a progression of changes until his mind is at rest at the same time the material is right. [p. 148]

Here I take the liberty of adapting Pirsig's description of how a master repairs a machine to Monty Roberts's horse-training method.

Monty isn't ever following a single line of instruction. He's making decisions as he goes along. For that reason, he'll be absorbed and attentive to what he is doing. His motions are in a kind of harmony with the horse. He isn't following any set of written instructions because the horse's state determines what Monty thinks and does. What Monty thinks and does then further shapes the state of the horse, which, in turn, further shapes Monty's actions. In all of this there is ever-increasing trust. The quality of the relationship between Monty and the horse is changing. The two are in a dynamic relationship that is giving rise to a capacity that neither has individually. Each relationship with each horse is not exactly like any previous relationship. But there is a desired outcome and general principles that Monty follows until the outcome is co-created.

What is common to the mastery of machines, or horses, and the changing of human systems? Let's adapt the description to a skilled executive trying to change a group of people.

The executive isn't ever following a single line of instruction. She is making decisions as she goes along. For that reason she'll be absorbed and attentive to what she is doing. She and the people are in a kind of harmony. The state of the group determines what she thinks and does. What she thinks and does then further shapes the state of the people, which in turn further shapes the executive. In all of this there is ever-increasing trust. The quality of the relationship between the executive and her group is changing. The two are in a dynamic relationship that is giving rise to a capacity that cannot otherwise exist. This relationship is not exactly like any previous relationship. But there is a desired outcome and general principles that she follows until the outcome is co-created.

Think About It

- Have you ever known someone who seemed to have a deeper understanding than others of how to improve the people around him or her? What sorts of things did this person do?

_____

_____

_____

TRAPPED IN NORMAL CHANGE ASSUMPTIONS

Monty Roberts was excited to share the many benefits that came from his new way of "gentling" horses with his father and other trainers. But they ignored the evidence and denied the validity of his claims, even after his methods won acclaim. How could these men reject a method that was so efficient and effective?

The answer is that they were men of another paradigm. They made normal assumptions. Horses were the enemy, and they were dangerous, so a trainer had to control the training process. The trainer achieved success by breaking the horse's will—by forcing the horse to comply. Their assumptions led to violence that only confirmed those assumptions. The idea of establishing a gentle, trusting relationship with a horse was so foreign to them that they could not make sense of Monty's method, much less attempt it themselves.

Most of us have similar internalized assumptions. When we need to influence others, we assume that we should tell them why they should change. We assume that we have greater expertise; we place ourselves in a position of superiority and attempt to exert control. We assume that we have the right to act upon others. If the people we hope to change do not comply, we look for points of leverage.

Leverage is the method we use to "break" the will of the other. Leverage produces resistance, and that resistance confirms our assumption that we need to be in control and crush the opposition. Having confirmed our assumptions, we reject any alternatives. To the horse breakers, Monty was a fool, and no hard evidence was going to change their conclusion. Their position had little to do with Monty; rather, it was the result of how their own identities had evolved. They sensed that Monty's method was better than theirs, and they felt threatened. Instead of embracing change, they held more tightly to their own assumptions. That is our normal way of reacting. We are those horse breakers. When we see evidence that suggests our core assumptions are wrong, we often ignore it or attempt to discredit it, because the suggestion that we need to learn stimulates feelings of fear.

When you develop the kind of adaptive confidence that Monty developed, you will be willing to accept evidence that contradicts your core assumptions. People with adaptive confidence are confident precisely because they know that they will incorporate new information into their plans, even when that new information requires them to change. Over time they begin to trust the fact that they can learn, that they can figure it out. They become confident that they can adapt.

Think About It

- Have you ever worked with anyone who refused to consider alternatives to their assumptions, despite the evidence? Why do you think the person did that? What was the result?

  _____

  _____

  _____

- What assumptions do you have about how to influence change in others? How successful have those assumptions been in effecting change?

  _____

  _____

  _____

- Considering the stories you have just read, what sorts of things could you do to improve your ability to adapt to different or changing circumstances?

_____

_____

_____

THE FAILURE OF SUCCESS

It is not easy to learn your way into a new assumption set. Some illustrations may help.

Bill was hired as a senior executive by a fast-growing company. He was excited about his new job but troubled by the fact that a few members of the hiring committee believed he did not have the requisite abilities. Wanting to prove that he was the right man for the job, he made a commitment to work harder than he had ever worked in his life. His commitment paid off. Within a short time, everyone agreed that Bill was the right choice.

Over the next several years, Bill noted that the harder he worked, the more recognition he received. He felt great satisfaction in his work and in the contributions he was making. This led him to work even harder. He was on an upward trajectory.

One day, Bill's wife expressed serious concern about his lifestyle. He was leaving for work at 4 A.M. and not returning home until late at night. Bill listened patiently but made little change. When confronted a second time, Bill promised not to leave for work until after breakfast and to be home in time for dinner. But he began working out of his briefcase from 4 A.M. until breakfast and from the end of dinner until it was time for bed.

Bill also noticed that his coworkers were sending subtle signals of displeasure. His performance was falling off and he was becoming more caustic. He felt trapped. His sense of ascent was gone. He was now on a downward trajectory.

One of Bill's associates suggested that he attend a retreat on the West Coast. He grudgingly agreed.

During the retreat, the participants were asked to draw a picture of something on the beach. Gazing around, Bill sat down to draw a picture of the withered, dying old pine tree in the dunes.

On the last day, the participants were asked to create an object that represented the week. Halfheartedly, Bill picked up a small log with a split in it and stuck a tumbleweed in the split. Holding up his creation, he caustically said, "Here is my week."

Suddenly he was struck by how much the tumbleweed resembled the dying pine tree he had drawn, and he was overwhelmed by a powerful insight. "I realized that I was that dying old pine tree and that I was denying my need for nourishment of the self."

In that moment Bill had an expanded consciousness. He could see his old self from outside his old self. He could see that his assumptions were responsible for his own downward trajectory.

Here is what he realized: As he attacked his challenging new job, he had grown and developed. For a time, there was a feedback loop between his efforts and his energy level. It was a self-reinforcing virtuous cycle; the more he worked, the more successful he became. At some point, however, his efforts began to bring diminishing returns. The virtuous cycle became a self-reinforcing vicious cycle. The harder he worked, the less effective his efforts, so he worked harder, thus becoming even less effective.

Often, when we find ourselves in situations that require us to adapt, we choose instead to distort reality, to deny what the world is telling us. Like the horse breakers, we hold tightly to our assumptions and tend to work harder within them when they are challenged.

Psychologists tell us that as our stress level increases, our attention span tends to diminish. We seek to solve new problems with the same methods by which we solved old problems. Instead of responding creatively, we increase our commitment to old patterns. At the very moment when innovative action is most needed, we implement our most ingrained response. To adapt, we must change our assumptions, but to do that we must have the courage to move forward, trusting that we can learn in real time.

Think About It

- Have you ever been in a position where your normal way of doing things stopped producing good results? How did you react?

- At a time when you were under stress and pressure, did anyone suggest ways you might be able to change yourself? What did you think of those suggestions?

BREAKING THE LOGIC OF TASK PURSUIT

Bill was following something we might call the *logic of task pursuit*. The logic of task pursuit is a mindset best illustrated by an old management parable.

A hermit would cut enough wood each summer to heat his forest cabin through the winter. One day, he heard on his shortwave radio that an early winter storm was heading his way. He rushed to his woodpile.

Examining his dull and rusty saw, he realized that it needed sharpening. Worried about the approaching storm, however, he began to cut. As he worked, he noted that the saw was getting increasingly dull and that he was working harder and harder. He told himself repeatedly that he needed to stop and sharpen the saw, but he continued to cut. As the snow began to fall, he sat exhausted next to a sizable pile of uncut wood.

This man was not ignorant. He knew his saw desperately needed sharpening. He also knew that the more he cut, the duller the blade would become. Yet, like Bill, he could not bring himself to stop and sharpen the saw. He was trapped in his routines and distracted by stress.

For most of us, when we are under pressure the pursuit of our immediate task drives out any thought of employing an alternative strategy. Careful planning becomes less important than keeping busy. I refer to it as the "tyranny of the in-basket"—the illusion that we have too much to do to take the time necessary to do what we really need to do.

Think About It

- How often do you, or the people around you, use busy-ness as an excuse to avoid important changes? Why?

_____

_____

_____

- Have you ever realized you needed to make a change, but chose not to because you felt as if there wasn't enough time? Do you think you were being honest with yourself? What was the result?

_____

_____

_____

- Our individual drive toward task completion often hides the need for deep change. How might you find time to work on necessary personal changes?

_____

_____

_____

The logic of task pursuit affects organizations as well as individuals. An organization is a collective entity that exists to accomplish specific tasks. Every organization is a group of systems—a cultural system, a strategic system, a technical system, and a political system. In an environment of constant change, each of these systems—like the hermit's saw—tends to become less efficient over time.

When an organization discovers that its systems need realignment, I am often asked to make a diagnosis. Senior executives seldom argue with my diagnosis, but they almost always argue with my recommendations. Often I am told, "What you don't understand is that we don't have the time to make the deep change you are recommending." This statement is supposedly about time. It is not. It is about work avoidance. Deep change is adaptive work. It requires that we learn to do things we do not know how to do. Learning to do new things in real time is frightening. It is like asking a horse trainer to learn a new way to gentle a horse or suggesting that Bill balance his life.

Like most people, executives prefer to stay where they are comfortable. But they need an excuse to do so. "We have no time" neutralizes personal responsibility. That mentality lets the executive trade deep change now for a crisis that will occur in the future. Yet confronting a future crisis appears far more desirable than making a deep change now. It could take years for the crisis to occur, and by then the executive might be somewhere else. Making deep change is risky, and few executives are willing to introduce the possibility of failure.

Like the hermit and the senior executives, most of us tend to ignore warning signals that suggest a need for change. As performance levels fall, our stress goes up, and our vitality and drive wane. Our focus narrows, and we increase our commitment to existing strategies, making it difficult to change. To avoid the experience of feeling stuck, we must have a change in consciousness. We have to make a deep change.

In the chapters that follow, you will learn to transcend your normal assumptions and make the shift toward increased consciousness. If you read carefully and think deeply, as you listen to the voice of your own conscience you will begin to get outside yourself and see that your assumptions and strategies do not match the actual context in which you are embedded. If you reflect on times when you were at your best, you will be filled with positive emotions that will give you the energy to reexamine your motives and discover how to live in a more committed way. When you make this realignment, your fears will be replaced with confidence. When you are committed to your highest purpose, you will move forward through the fear of conflict, and you will begin to live in a generative state of learning and contribution. Instead of repeating what you have done in the past, you will find a new way. You will learn how to make deep change at the personal level and how to make deep change at the collective level. You will become like Monty Roberts, able to change the emerging future by acting with that future. You will become a master of the deep change process.

Personal Reflection and Application

REFLECT

While the chapter is fresh in your mind, quickly write down the 4 to 6 points, concepts, or ideas that most stand out for you.

WATCH A FILM: *NORMA RAE*

In this film, we see a man named Reuben change an organization. He does this by mentoring a woman named Norma Rae through the process of deep personal change. As she moves forward she has to make new assumptions about who she is and what she can do. In the process she is transformed and she becomes a leader.

Questions to Consider

1. Normal relationships are based on expectations of exchange (I give you something and you give me something in return).

   • What was the expected exchange between Norma Rae and each of the following people or groups?

   Her lover

   _____

   _____

   _____

   Her father

   _____

   _____

   _____

Her boss

_____

_____

_____

Her peers

_____

_____

_____

Her fiancé

_____

_____

_____

- How did these external expectations determine the expectations Norma Rae had for herself?

_____

_____

_____

- What important external expectations determine the expectations you have for yourself?

_____

_____

_____

2. Extraordinary relationships transcend the norms of exchange.
   - What did you find to be Reuben's most surprising statements to or actions toward Norma Rae?

_____

_____

_____

- How is Reuben different from the other people in Norma Rae's life?

  _____

  _____

  _____

- What did Reuben do to help Norma Rae become a transformational leader?

  _____

  _____

  _____

- Have you ever influenced people the way that Reuben influenced Norma Rae?

  _____

  _____

  _____

3. After being fired, Norma Rae walks through the factory and then jumps up on the table and holds up a sign with the word *Union* on it. This was her defining moment.

   - How did Norma Rae know that holding up the sign would work? When did she plan the process?

     _____

     _____

     _____

   - What are some transformational moments you have witnessed?

     _____

     _____

     _____

4. Norma Rae's husband tells Reuben that Norma Rae has changed and he does not like it. Reuben responds, "She stood up on a table. She's a free woman. Maybe you can live with it, maybe you can't."

- Explain what Reuben meant. What does it have to do with becoming a leader of deep change?

  _____

  _____

  _____

- Can you think of a time when you felt powerful and free?

  _____

  _____

  _____

- Do you believe you can be powerful and free? Why or why not? What does this belief have to do with your capacity to lead?

  _____

  _____

  _____

5. This film is about Norma Rae's transformation, but it is also about organizational change.

   - What did you learn from the film about the connection between individual change and organizational change?

     _____

     _____

     _____

   - What key connections do you see between the movie and the concepts in this chapter?

     _____

     _____

     _____

6. List the key insights you gained from the movie and briefly describe life experiences that you associate with these insights.

_____

_____

_____

7. A very effective way to learn about deep change is to mentor someone through the deep change process. Before you begin Chapter Two, prepare yourself to take on the assignment of becoming a transformational mentor like Reuben. Who will you work with?

_____

_____

_____

MAKE A JOURNAL ENTRY

Read the following statements. Check the 2 or 3 that resonate most with you.

____1. Research reveals that 50 percent of all organizational change initiatives fail.

____2. We are trapped in our assumption that hierarchy, control, linearity, expertise, achievement, and recognition are the best measures of success.

____3. We often find ourselves in situations that require us to adapt, but choose to distort reality and deny what the world is telling us.

____4. To adapt we must change our assumptions, but to change our assumptions we must have the courage to leave our comfort zone and move forward, experimenting and paying attention to feedback in real time.

____5. We can only be excellent if we are not doing what is normal; to be excellent, we have to be at the edge, a place of uncertainty and learning.

____6. When we become a more effective version of ourselves, we become empowered individuals and more empowering members of our community.

____7. Assumptions of hierarchy become latent as people learn together in networks of equality.

___8. A master of deep change tends to have a universal theory of change, believing that he or she can bring about a transformation in nearly any situation.

___9. If we try reaching back, reflecting on when we were at our best, we will be filled with positive emotions and find the energy to reexamine our motives and live in a more committed way.

___10. When we are committed to our highest purpose, we move forward through the fear of conflict, and begin to live in a generative state of learning and contribution.

Now circle the number of the single statement you most resonate with. List some life experiences that you associate with that statement. Then write a paragraph that expresses the importance of one of those life experiences.

Life experiences:

_____

_____

_____

Paragraph:

_____

_____

_____

WRITE A MEMO

Based on your insights, your responses to the questions about the film, and your journal entry, write a short note to someone you know. Help the person understand the essence of what you have learned in this chapter.

_____

_____

_____

_____

_____

APPLY THE LEARNING

What are one or two actions you will take from what you have learned in this chapter to get started on your journey of mastering the deep change process?

_____

_____

_____

_____

_____

CHAPTER TWO

EXPERIENCING SLOW DEATH

IN THIS CHAPTER

- Organizations must constantly change.
- Executives often practice denial.
- Organizations and people regularly fall into the pattern of slow death.
- The way out of slow death is deep change.

Decades ago, I was invited to a meeting of senior officers at a military academy. The general in charge talked at length about the moral decay in society. It turned out that some of the students at the academy were cheating on their exams, and the officers believed that corruption in society was to blame. They argued that by the time some eighteen-year-olds arrived at the academy they were irredeemable.

After a long discussion, I asked whether anyone in the room had served in Vietnam. Most did serve in Vietnam. I asked whether any of them had participated in the phenomenon known as the body count. This was a measurement system used to determine how American forces were performing by counting enemy deaths after each battle. The numbers were often vastly exaggerated.

From the discomfort in the room, it was clear that they were all aware of the issue. Why, I asked, would a commissioned officer engage in such behavior?

Answering my own question, I told them of the day in officer basic training when my company did poorly on a test. Our performance reflected badly on the staff, and the master sergeant came in and told us to "cooperate and graduate"—meaning that we should share answers so that everyone would pass. In other words, the army taught me to cheat. I suggested that, in a large hierarchy, people often experience pressure to engage in unethical behaviors so that everyone will look good. I then raised a question: Is it possible that there is a system here that requires the cadets to cheat, teaches them to cheat, and rewards them for cheating?

There was a very long silence. Finally, the officer in charge turned to the officer next to him, and as if I had never said a word, resumed the old discussion about moral decay in society. For the rest of the day, the officers ignored me.

Think About It

- Why were the officers so uncomfortable with the mention of the body count?

_____

_____

_____

- Have you ever been in an organization where the leaders blamed problems on things outside of their control? Why did they do that? What was the result?

_____

_____

_____

- How would you react if you were the officer in charge?

_____

_____

_____

DENIAL LEADS TO SLOW DEATH

The behavior of those officers was not surprising. We all tend to be just like them. When someone suggests that we play a role in creating a problem and might need to change, we often respond by doing what the officers did: we practice denial.

Denial is a normal reaction. We often resort to denial when we are presented with painful information about ourselves, especially when the information suggests that we need to make a deep change.

It is important to understand denial because it often leads to the *slow death* of organizations and individuals. When we practice denial, we work on the wrong things and ignore signs that our strategies are ineffective. Like Bill in the last chapter, we work hard, but the underlying problem tends to grow worse while we become increasingly discouraged. This leads to hopelessness. The people in the organization begin to disengage from the organizational good to pursue their own good. Conflicts intensify and more problems surface, eventually reaching a tipping point. The process of slow death becomes fast death.

I seldom visit an organization free from some form of slow death. Because slow death is so common, it is crucial that we understand the concept and learn how we can make a difference from within a normal, slowly dying system.

When I think of slow death, I think of something I saw while visiting a company. I was walking down a long hallway in a room where hundreds of people were working. The place felt lifeless—people seemed reluctant to be there, spoke in low tones, and moved slowly, as if they were dragging heavy weights behind them. My companion seemed to read my mind as she remarked, "Here we house the legions of the walking dead."

It is not unusual to find people who are not engaged in their work, who feel meaningless and hopeless. In the words of Thoreau, they are living lives of "quiet desperation." Quiet desperation is one of the symptoms of slow death that many people recognize. When I share this image of the walking dead, people commonly say, "Yes, there are many people like that, and it is unfortunate that they are the way they are."

But we are *all* participants in the slow death process. When we become aware of the process, we need to understand and stop it. Otherwise, we contribute to its spread.

Think About It

• Have you ever visited an organization that seemed to be filled with unhappy employees who had little reason to care about their work? How did it feel to be there?

_____

_____

_____

- Have you ever been part of an organization that had fallen as deeply into the slow death process as the one described in the preceding paragraphs? What kinds of things did people do that contributed to the overall feeling of lifelessness? What were employees' attitudes toward one another? How did superiors treat the people below them? How did the atmosphere affect you?

_____

_____

_____

THE SOURCE OF SLOW DEATH

Today, in a world of constant change, we see slow death more often. It is not easy to maintain faith, courage, and energy in today's world. Having to face the endless challenges of organizational life can corrode our motivation and initiative. Consider the following statements by senior executives at two different organizations who were facing the prospect of making a major change they did not want to make:

> I've been in this position for four years, and every year the work pressure has increased. I'm fifty-seven, and I'm doing all I can to hold on. I know we need to implement this thing. I just don't think we can do one more major change.
>
> From a long-run perspective, there is no choice. But to tell you the truth, I'm not sure I have it in me. Of the eight vice presidents, three are simply not up to taking this on. We're all around the same age, and we're all thinking, "If I can hang in just a couple of more years, this problem will belong to someone else." The issue is not what's good in the long run; it's how to survive right now.

Like the military officers, these executives are not bad people. They are normal people doing the natural thing. Yet it is important to be clear. Although both executives recognize that a deep change is needed in their organization, both seem to have opted for personal reasons not to make the needed change. They are putting their own good ahead of the organizational good. By avoiding making the change, they are contributing to the process of slow death in their organizations. The disease they might readily condemn in others is a disease they carry and spread.

Think About It

- Have you ever worked for a person who was avoiding a change that was in the best interests of the organization? How did it influence you?

  _____

  _____

  _____

- Have you ever done the same?

  _____

  _____

  _____

HOW SLOW DEATH UNFOLDS

On the following pages, six managers describe how the slow death process unfolded in their organizations.

Manager #1

We chose slow death three years ago. The organization gave up a significant position in the industry because of an internal conflict between divisions with opposing philosophies. We needed real change, and everyone knew it. Yet no one was willing to engage it. The result was that we went from thirty-one thousand people to fewer than fifteen thousand in a two-year period. We are no longer a significant player, and there is no hope for the future. It is now just a matter of time.

I seldom do an organizational diagnosis without finding at least one example of intergroup conflict. It is often ignored because no one can imagine how to transform the conflict into collaboration. Yet transforming conflict into collaboration is the essence of leadership. In this executive's case the conflict gave rise to the slow death process, and the absence of real leadership allowed it to grow into the need for major downsizing.

Manager #2

> Slow death is what we are about—a conservative, "Don't rock the boat" culture: executives three to five years from retirement, little long-range planning, no vision, and denial of all external criticism. We make superficial changes . . . but we make no real change in our basic structures and processes. We are on a course that is clear to all.

Large hierarchies are a natural seedbed for the emergence of a conservative culture. Constructive disagreement is a sign of organizational health, but in conservative cultures criticism is often stifled. A climate of constructive conflict indicates effective leadership. In this case the manager's last sentence is an interesting one. He points out that everyone recognizes where the organization is probably headed: first to a crisis, then to the same downsizing process mentioned in the first case.

Manager #3

> As a member of a top-management team, I experienced the slow death of a major corporation ten years ago. We . . . resisted change until we were forced to engage an entire series of wild and uncoordinated changes. Finally, we went through a slow painful death. It was a merger that few of our people survived. Now I'm experiencing it all over again. It is a haunting case of, "Hey, I've been here before."

Here we see another conservative culture that was impervious to change. The manager notes a pattern that is often a part of the slow death process, the shift to "wild and uncoordinated changes." With this shift, slow death tends to turn into fast death, at which point it is usually too late to turn things around; the organization is so weakened that it dies. Note that this observer, a top manager, has seen the process before, and is watching it unfold once again.

Manager #4

We are dying. In the meantime, my boss goes around reducing everything to numbers and charts. He leaves the real task of leadership to others. Because we no longer believe in the organization's future, we're all tending to our own personal futures. I would love to be thinking about constructive alternatives, but it's simply too late.

Here we see the difference between management and leadership. Organizations need people who can actually lead the deep change process. This means reaching hearts as well as heads.

Note that there is a point in the process of slow death when people give up on the pursuit of the organizational good and simply begin to take care of themselves. This is a sure sign of the slow death process. It is a common occurrence in human collectives.

Manager #5

I think our company has about twelve to eighteen months, and then it will be too late. To be truly competitive, we have to alter the underlying system. That means, however, getting past the ever-present and undeniably important daily tasks. It means doing more. I think we keep busy because it is a kind of opium. We don't know how to confront the deep change process, so we keep ourselves busy with the normal stuff and try not to notice what's really happening. I'm not optimistic. There is no vision from the top, and the changes continue to be incremental. As I see it, we are very clearly choosing slow death.

A change in the underlying system of an organization is usually a very big change. It is not only technological but also political, and therefore full of potential conflict. In this case, "doing more" means dealing with the underlying system, but people are unwilling to do so. Instead, they stay busy. Note that staying busy is "a kind of opium." The logic of task pursuit acts like a drug that dulls people and helps them avoid the work of deep change needed to turn the company around.

Manager #6

Our top management people are ill-equipped to deal with the realities of our situation. We need sweeping changes. Their tools, obtained at the best business schools, are simply inadequate for facing our current competitive environment. They know how to manage, not how to lead. Besides, it is too late. We cannot be saved by willing it, even from the top. It's like trying to find a golf swing the day before the Masters.

In the process of slow death people lose faith in their leaders. This occurs because people in leadership positions tend to resort to control and the processes of normal management. But they need to do the opposite: to learn, to envision, to join with their people in the process of deep change. Because they continue to follow normal practices, they lose crucial time. When the moment of crisis arrives, the organization does not have the characteristics it needs for survival. It is too late.

Think About It

- What do the executives' statements have in common? What patterns do you see in those stories? What keeps happening again and again? Why?

- Are any of these patterns familiar? Have you experienced them in your own organizations? What could you or other leaders have done to halt the process of slow death and turn it around?

_____

_____

_____

CHARACTERISTICS OF THE SLOW DEATH PROCESS

Here are some of the patterns you might have recognized in these six stories.

Goal inversion: External environments continually change. Organizations, however, are structured by assumptions based on previous experience. Rather than change in response to new expectations and demands, people act their way into a new goal: to serve the needs of others in the organization rather than those of the customers or clients.

Conflict: A change in external demands has implications for internal politics. The slow death process is often linked to some organizational conflict that is being ignored or covered up by leaders who do not know how to transform conflict into collaboration.

Denial: Denial is one way to avoid conflict. The most difficult problems that emerge in an organization often have political implications. I might know that the boss has no idea how to deal with a given conflict, and that self-interest leads him or her to ignore it. Because my own self-interest is best served by not antagonizing the boss, I remain silent. Together we collude to deny the problem. This "dance" is a central dynamic in slow death.

Abdication: A variation on the denial theme is the abdication of leadership. People point fingers and articulate blame but they do not take responsibility. Everyone hungers for a vision that inspires and integrates, but no one knows how to find one. In the absence of a meaningful vision, people lose hope and become defensive. They begin to point fingers, sending blame up, across, and down the organization. Everyone becomes disempowered.

Posturing: When trust dies and people pursue self-interest, their communication ceases to be authentic, and learning slows. Yet people in positions of authority are expected to know the truth and have an effective strategy. Because they cannot do this in an inauthentic environment, they begin to posture—for example, to call for new outcomes while refusing to engage in new behaviors. Such posturing makes authentic communication difficult.

Excuses: As you have already learned, a major excuse for not making deep change is time. People justify their behavior patterns by saying that they lack the time to get involved in a significant change effort. To use an old analogy, this is like rearranging the deck chairs on the *Titanic* as it goes down. By keeping busy with everyday tasks, people distract themselves from the important but unsettling truth: the ship is sinking.

Chaos: Slow death often reaches a tipping point and becomes fast death. At the tipping point, people engage in a series of last-ditch, wild and uncoordinated change efforts in an attempt to avoid disaster. It is a death dance performed by horrified people in terrifying circumstances.

ORGANIZING AS A LIVING SYSTEM

Many of us think of an organization as a machine-like object. Yet it is often more fruitful to think of an organization as a living system that has a trajectory: it is either gaining or losing energy. According to the second law of thermodynamics, unless work is done to the contrary, a system tends to close down and move toward entropy, or the loss of energy.

A key phrase is *unless work is done to the contrary*. The work that turns the organizational trajectory upward is called *leadership*. A leader overcomes the slow death of an organization by transcending his or her assumptions and then getting others to do the same.

A useful illustration of organizational death and rebirth is found in a book cowritten by Kim S. Cameron and myself: *Diagnosing and Changing Organizational Culture* (2011). The case begins in the 1950s and continues over several decades. It concerns the transformation of an auto assembly plant in Fremont, California. Here's a summary:

In the 1950s, General Motors embarked on what was referred to as a "sunbelt strategy": plants were built in southern and western states. Because these were all states where unions were not allowed to require that new workers become union members, the United Auto Workers (UAW) viewed this as a union-avoidance move. When the UAW eventually organized at the plants, they became among the most hostile, conflict-ridden plants in GM's entire corporation.

The Fremont plant was particularly troublesome. By 1982, the plant was operating at a disastrously low level, with high absenteeism, disgruntled employees, and wildcat strikes. Costs were 30 percent above those of GM's Japanese competitors, sales were trending downward, and the plant was at the very bottom of companywide quality and productivity rankings. Moreover, customer satisfaction with the Chevy Nova, which was built in Fremont, had hit rock bottom.

A variety of improvement programs had been attempted, but nothing worked. The reputation of the entire corporation was being negatively affected, the operating costs were overly burdensome, and management had nothing but grief from the employees. The decision was made to close the plant.

Then GM did something interesting. The company approached a competitor, Toyota, with an offer to collaborate on designing and building a car. Toyota jumped at the chance. After all, GM was the world's largest company, had the world's largest supplier and dealer networks, and was giving Toyota a chance to establish a firm footing on U.S. soil. GM offered the use of the Fremont facility, but the plant was not to be remodeled. Toyota said, "Fine." UAW workers had to be hired back first, on the basis of seniority. The oldest and most recalcitrant employees, those who had complained about management the longest, were given first crack at jobs. Toyota said, "Fine." Toyota had just one request: to allow Toyota managers to run the place. GM said, "Fine."

Approximately a year and a half after being shuttered, the plant was reopened with a new name: NUMMI—New United Motors Manufacturing Incorporated. Everything improved—employee satisfaction, sales trends, quality, productivity, and customer satisfaction.

What accounts for this dramatic improvement in performance? The most important factor was described by a production employee who had worked in the GM facility for more than twenty years. He said that prior to the joint venture, he would go home at night chuckling to himself about the things he had thought up during the day to mess up the system. He'd leave his sandwich behind the door panel of a car, for example. "A month later, the customer would be driving down the road and wouldn't be able to figure out where that terrible smell was coming from.

This employee's job was to monitor robots that spot-welded parts of the frame together. "Now," he commented, "because the number of job classifications has been so dramatically reduced [from more than 150 to 8], we have all been allowed to have business cards and to make up our own job titles. The title I put on my card is 'Director of Welding Improvement.' When I see a Toyota Corolla in a parking lot, I leave a business card under the windshield wiper with a note: 'I made your car. Any problems, call me.' I do it because I feel personally responsible for those cars."

The plant continued for years. In 2009 GM pulled out of the joint venture. In 2010 the plant became a cooperative effort between Tesla Motors and Toyota.

Think About It

- What key changes do you imagine must have taken place within the plant once the Toyota managers took over?

  _____

  _____

  _____

- Consider the "Director of Welding Improvement" who placed his business card on Corollas he saw parked around him. What kind of atmosphere in your organization would cause you to take as much pride in your work? How could you contribute to building that kind of culture?

  _____

  _____

  _____

DEEP CHANGE

There are so many things to be learned from the GM case. Yet there is one point that towers over all others: the GM plant at Fremont was a human system teeming with potential. The executives were so firm in their conclusions about the lack of potential that they, in essence, gave the plant away. The people from Toyota, by contrast, could see the potential. They built their efforts on two pillars: commitment to continuous improvement and respect for people. They recognized that the problem lay in the plant's culture. They therefore set about making deep change, working to change the culture by giving each employee a personal stake in the product he or she produced. The change process was not dictatorial. It was an effort in mutual learning. Like Monty Roberts, the Toyota leaders had the capacity to engage and "gentle" the horses that could not be broken. They could turn slow death into deep change.

When most of us talk about change, we usually mean the type of incremental change that results from a rational analysis and planning process, with a desired goal and a specific set of steps for reaching it. Incremental change is usually limited in scope and often reversible; if the change does not work out, we can always return to the old way. It does not disrupt the patterns we have learned from our past experiences—it is an extension of the past. When we are making incremental changes, we feel as if we are in control.

As we saw in Chapter One, deep change differs from incremental change because it requires real-time engagement and learning, new assumptions, and new ways of thinking and behaving. Whereas incremental change is contained, consistent, and reversible, deep change is major in scope, discontinuous with the past, and usually irreversible. It is based on assumptions of possibility. The cultural shift at the Fremont plant is an example: the Toyota leaders set about actualizing the potential that the GM leaders could not see.

The deep change process involves taking risks and learning how to live in new ways. Like Monty's horse-training method, it requires mutuality and interdependence, even in areas normally dominated by power relationships and forced change efforts. Because the learning process is interactive, it cannot be controlled, only influenced. Further, we must interact with the change process. Through this interaction we experience the regeneration and reenergizing of the organization. The more we do this, the more we understand that we are actually "making it up" as we go along.

One of the most elusive aspects of deep change is that it begins with self-change. The process begins when we see reality as it is, which requires resisting the desire to engage in denial and being open to the possibility that we need to change. If we leaders can change the quality of our selves, the relationships around us will improve. When this happens the system generates new collective capacities.

ON SEEING ME AS I REALLY AM

I have a friend named Ellen Toronto who is a clinical psychologist. One day I was talking about the deep change process when she made a comment that captured my full attention. Here is what she said:

> At the personal level, I deal with this issue every day. Every time a client comes to me with a problem, what I find is that the person is experiencing slow death. What I try to help such persons see is that they have a choice. They can continue to experience slow death, or they can make a deep change. Most do not have the courage to engage the process of deep change, and so most are not cured. The challenge is to provide people with enough encouragement, help, and support that they dare to try.

Individuals go to see people like Ellen because they hope to escape the slow death process they are experiencing at the personal level. She helps us see that we can escape our pain if we want to. Yet we may actually prefer the pain of slow death because we tend to prefer the devil we know. The alternative is self-modification or deep change, which requires discipline, courage, motivation, and a willingness to seek new experiences. It suggests profound learning. It requires altering the assumptions on which our present identity is based, and the thought of challenging those assumptions makes most of us very uncomfortable. When we realize how much work is involved in making a change, it may suddenly seem easier to continue enduring our current troubles.

When I first started exploring the subject of slow death, I saw it as an organizational process. Ellen confirmed my growing suspicion that it is very much a personal issue, and that it is far more basic and common than I originally thought. I realized that everyone has the tendency to choose slow death, including me. That realization was very painful. I became fascinated by all the ways in which I could deny the fact that I was sometimes lazy or lacked courage. But I began to realize that if I was not growing, I was dying.

Think About It

- In your experience, are people more likely to choose to change themselves or to stick with what they are already doing, even if they are unhappy doing it? Why?

- Have you ever been faced with a choice either to make significant changes or to face unpleasant but familiar consequences? Which did you choose? Why did you make that choice? What were the results?

_____

_____

_____

- Have you been thinking about making a personal change but feeling hesitant or reluctant to do so? What might convince you to go ahead? What kind of support would you need? How might you get it?

_____

_____

_____

Personal Reflection and Application

REFLECT

While the chapter is fresh in your mind, quickly write down the 4 to 6 points, concepts, or ideas that stand out for you the most.

WATCH THE FILM: *MONEYBALL*

Moneyball is a story of deep change. In 2002, Billy Beane, the general manager of the Oakland Athletics, lost three stars to free agency. His small budget made it impossible for him to comply with the normal assumptions of how to build a winning team. Searching for alternatives, he became open to new ways of thinking. He started a journey that ended up revolutionizing the sport. The story helps us understand the deep change process in all organizations.

Questions to Consider

1. What was good about losing three star players and not being able to replace them?

   _____

   _____

   _____

2. How does this generalize to other situations?

   _____

   _____

   _____

3. On the journey of deep change people often make surprising discoveries. How did Beane find Paul DePodesta? Why did he hire DePodesta? Why was DePodesta able to thrive in this new environment?

   _____

   _____

   _____

4. Why did Beane believe that DePodesta's theory could provide a competitive advantage?

   _____

   _____

   _____

5. Who fought hardest against the changes made by Beane and DePodesta? Why? Did the scouting team have anything in common with the horse trainers described in Chapter One?

   _____

   _____

   _____

6. As the new season began, the team's performance was awful. Criticism and social pressure built. What kept Beane from caving in?

    _____

    _____

    _____

7. In the middle of the season, Beane made some surprising trades. Why? How do they relate to the idea that deep change is a learning process?

    _____

    _____

    _____

8. When Beane visited Boston, John Henry, the owner of the Red Sox, described the deep change process in any organization or industry. What were his key points? Why did Beane not accept the Red Sox offer?

    _____

    _____

    _____

9. Many of Beane's decisions are related to his experience as a failed player. What can his experiences teach us about the role of failure in the change process?

    _____

    _____

    _____

10. Think about your commitment to become a transformational mentor to a specific person or persons. What additional tools do you find in the movie?

    _____

    _____

    _____

MAKE A JOURNAL ENTRY

Read the following statements. Check the 2 or 3 that resonate most with you.

___1. We often resort to denial when we are presented with painful information about ourselves that suggests that we need to make a deep change.

___2. When we practice denial, we work on the wrong things and continue using ineffective strategies. Then the underlying problem tends to grow worse and we become discouraged.

___3. By staying busy with everyday tasks, people are able to distract themselves from the truth that their ship is sinking.

___4. There is a point in the process of slow death when people give up on pursuing the organizational good and simply begin taking care of themselves. They act their way into a new goal, which is to serve their own needs, not the needs of the customers or clients.

___5. Most organizations suffer from some kind of intergroup conflict that is ignored or covered up by authority figures who do not know how to transform the conflict into collaboration.

___6. When we all know we cannot talk about a key issue, we tend to lose confidence in the people around us and become increasingly isolated; there are many individuals performing roles but there is no organization.

___7. Eventually we reach a tipping point, and the process of slow death becomes fast death.

___8. Transforming conflict into collaboration is the essence of leadership.

___9. The truth is that few executives know how to find a vision that inspires and integrates.

___10. In the absence of a meaningful vision, people lose hope.

Now circle the number of the single statement you most resonate with. List some life experiences that you associate with that statement. Then write a paragraph that expresses the importance of one of those life experiences.

Life experiences:

_____

_____

_____

Paragraph:

_____

_____

_____

WRITE A MEMO

Based on your insights, your responses to the questions about the film, and your journal entry, write a short note to someone you know to convey the essence of what you have learned in this chapter.

_____

_____

_____

_____

APPLY THE LEARNING

What are one or two actions you will take from what you have learned in this chapter as the next steps on your journey of mastering the deep change process?

_____

_____

_____

_____

CHAPTER THREE

THE POWER OF SELF-CHANGE

IN THIS CHAPTER

- Our own actions sometimes contribute to the problems we set out to solve.
- If we want our change efforts to succeed, we must learn to look at the world in new ways.
- Successful change efforts are led by people who have committed to changing themselves.
- Deep change begins with personal change.

I once worked with a company whose leaders had attended a well-known seminar on how to build a "quality culture." By this they meant that they would create a culture that valued the customer, provided high-quality products, and enabled relationships of respect and trust. They expected this change to result in greater profits, productivity, efficiency, morale, and innovation.

The executives had developed a reasonable plan and begun the change effort. A short time later, while we were working together on strategic planning, the team frequently referred to their work on the new quality culture. They were planning the future of their company around the premise that significant positive changes would happen. I told them about another company that had sent its senior executives to the same seminar. Three years later, however, they found that their new plan for dramatic improvements had made little, if any, impact.

The executives wanted to know, "Why did their attempts to create a quality culture fail?" Instead of explaining, I asked *them* to tell me why.

A heavy silence filled the room. Finally, one of the most influential members of the group said, "The leaders of the company didn't change their behavior."

I nodded. Then I challenged them: "Identify one time during your planning for a culture change when one of you said you were going to change your behavior." No one raised a hand.

There was a long pause. Something important and unusual was happening. These executives were suddenly seeing something that few people ever clearly see—the incongruity of asking for deep change in others while failing to commit to deep self-change. It was as if they were standing at the edge of a cliff and peering over. They decided to adjourn and think further about our discussion.

It's not surprising that these executives had not considered self-change when planning strategies for changing their company's culture. Like most executives, they felt about creating change in others the way that the horse breakers in Chapter One felt about breaking horses: they believed that change is the result of forceful leadership that imposes the will of an authority figure on resistant subordinates.

The belief that change must be imposed on one actor by another is one of our normal assumptions. This assumption is so deeply held that it blocks us from understanding one of the non-normal assumptions at the heart of leading deep change. That assumption is this: deep change begins with personal change.

Think About It

- Have you ever been a part of a group change effort? How well did that change effort succeed? What went well and what went poorly? Why, in your opinion, did things pan out the way they did?

_____

_____

_____

- Have you ever worked for a manager who expected you to change your behavior but did not make changes himself or herself? How did that feel? Did you change? If so, why? If not, why not?

_____

_____

_____

A GENERATIVE LEADER

The argument at the heart of my work is that self-change is crucial to leadership. For the organization to become a more adaptive system that is learning, the leader must become a more adaptive system who is learning.

When I teach this concept most people listen respectfully. Some are even deeply impressed, but few actually come to believe that self-change is the key to collective excellence. Again, the notion defies our normal assumptions. For this reason I look for people who exemplify the principle.

One such person is Andrea Jung, CEO of Avon. In a June 14, 2009, interview with _USA Today_, she talked about "fixing the roof while the sun is still shining." She was talking about being proactive, about making bold change. She argued that leaders need to see potential and pursue new opportunity, rather than simply react to problems as they arise.

Many people make the normal assumption that people in an organization will change only in a crisis—when the roof falls in during a storm. At the root of this belief is a second assumption—that people are reactive and resist change, and so must be forced into changing by some clear and present danger. A very different perspective holds that organizations are in fact full of potential, and that potential can be released through constant, positive, proactive change. People like Andrea Jung are able to see the latent potential that exists in organizations and they excel at realizing it.

But what does this have to do with self-change?

In the newspaper interview, Andrea Jung indicated that people with long experience sometimes cannot "look at the business with fresh eyes." Like the people at the failed GM plant (Chapter Two), they are so trapped in their assumptions that they cannot see the possibilities in the present. What, then, is an experienced senior executive to do?

Jung provided some extraordinary advice: "Fire yourself on a Friday night and come in on Monday morning as if a search firm put you there to be a turn-around leader. Can you be objective and make the bold change? If you can't, then you haven't reinvented yourself. I'm not the same leader I was even last year. . . . I've had to reinvent myself every year."

Jung is an executive who has come to understand the necessity for self-change. As CEO of a major corporation, she recognizes that she must continually change in order to lead, and she believes that all leaders would be more effective if they were always willing to make changes. People who are not changing tend to become trapped in their own assumptions. They naturally slip into the personal process of slow death. Those who are continually changing are also continually learning, continually challenging their own assumptions. Because they are changing, they have "fresh eyes" and can see the possibilities that others cannot.

Think About It

- What do you think about Andrea Jung's advice to fire yourself on Friday and come back on Monday as if a search firm had put you there to be a turnaround leader? Do you think that you could reevaluate your assumptions and shift your perspective that way? Why or why not?

  _____

  _____

  _____

- Have you ever had someone close to you make a deep personal change? What do you think prompted the person to make that change? What was the change, and what were the results?

  _____

  _____

  _____

LEVELS OF CHANGE

By advocating a fresh perspective and self-change, Andrea Jung calls on us to transcend past assumptions, live in the present, see potential, and then actualize it. This requires living in a heightened state of awareness. Firing ourselves on Friday automatically forces us to make new assumptions and stand in the present with proactive intent. In a proactive stance we can more productively orient ourselves toward the unfolding future. Instead of dragging our past baggage into the future, we bring the future into our pristine present, where we can shape what is unfolding. This is a transformational stance. It transforms our orientation from the past to the future, unlocking our generative capacities.

The transformational way of thinking was well-captured by Otto Scharmer in his book, *Theory U: Leading from the Future as It Emerges*. Scharmer distinguishes between different levels, or depths, of change, each of which demands more effort on the part of the leader. At the first level, the individual simply responds to outside stimuli, whereas the deepest level is reached only at the end of a long, careful process of self-examination. Ranked from easiest to most challenging, here are Scharmer's levels of change:

- *Re-acting:* A challenge confronts us and we try to resolve it.
- *Re-structuring:* We define current reality and decide to create new structures and processes.
- *Re-designing:* We recognize other ways of perceiving the challenge and we create new core activities and processes that incorporate our changed perspective.
- *Re-framing:* We engage in dialogue with the key actors, and the process reveals many of our own deep assumptions. Understanding our assumptions helps us create new thinking and new principles of action.
- *Re-generating:* We reexamine our purpose and discover where our commitment comes from. We draw strength from understanding why we do what we do.

Reacting

Most change is made at the *reactive* level. We perceive a problem and seek to solve it, attempting to restore equilibrium, to return things "back" to where they were.

We are not trying to create value; instead, we are trying to preserve it. In organizations, solving problems to maintain equilibrium often becomes equated with the role of manager. But this problem-solving mentality rewards conservative behavior. Senior leaders usually agree that they should be looking decades into the future, but then they describe the pressures they face and the constant flow of problems that need to be solved immediately. These "realities" are, in fact, very real. Because there is so much that needs to be done, leaders allow themselves to be pulled into a reactive stance. This is what Andrea Jung hoped to prevent when she "fired" herself so that she could change her perspective.

Restructuring

Restructuring is a common fact of organizational life. Although this is often done for good reason, sometimes it is done simply to avoid conflict, and the same problems that prompted the restructuring may reemerge six months later. Shuffling the boxes on the organizational chart looks like change but ignores the fact that, in many cases, the real problem is in the culture.

Redesigning

Redesigning is a deeper form of change. In the process of redesign, we may be exposed to new perceptions and gain important insights, leading us to do something like change a core technology or implement new activities and processes. Unfortunately, as with the managers discussed in Chapter One who tried unsuccessfully to implement Toyota's concept of lean manufacturing, holding onto normal assumptions will keep our change efforts from succeeding, no matter how many resources we invest.

Reframing

When we reach the level of reframing, we begin to approach deep change. Deep change is not about incremental change over which we have complete control. It involves adaptive change: the process of learning our way forward, and from our new experiences, developing new assumptions. At this level, we are "building the bridge as we walk on it." We join with others in ongoing dialogues and experiments, and this helps us identify and alter our assumptions. We begin to think in new ways, and we begin to follow new principles of action.

Regenerating

Reframing tends to happen alongside regeneration, the deepest level of change. In the earlier stages, we act by applying what we have already learned. We believe we are in control and that we know what to do, which often leads us to objectify the other people involved in the change process: our assumptions suggest that we may act upon them and that they should be passive recipients of our intentions.

In the process of regeneration our normal state of being shifts. We orient to a purpose that we truly value. To create an innovative result, we must become fully committed to that result. We must be willing to move toward it by learning our way into the creation of the result. Learning our way into the creation of a result means shedding our preconceptions and embracing what-ever new information presents itself—especially information about our own role in advancing or impeding the change process. In the process of deep change, we co-create the future by interacting with it as it emerges, learning in real time. Like the horse whisperer and the horse, two or more beings join in a new experience, and in the process of collective learning new outcomes emerge. In the process of learning and discovery we energize relationships and organizations while also regenerating ourselves.

Think About It

- Which one of Otto Scharmer's levels of change most closely describes the change you most frequently see in the groups and organizations around you?

  ____ *Reacting*

  ____ *Restructuring*

  ____ *Redesigning*

  ____ *Reframing*

  ____ *Regenerating*

- Why does change tend to happen at that level?

  _____

  _____

  _____

- What are the usual results?

  _____

  _____

  _____

- Can you recall a time when you acted at the reframing or regeneration levels in the face of a challenge? Briefly describe the situation.

  _____

  _____

  _____

  How did it feel to act at that level?

  _____

  _____

  _____

  How did your relationships change?

  _____

  _____

  _____

  What were the other results?

  _____

  _____

  _____

  What did you learn that you have been able to use moving forward?

  _____

  _____

  _____

  If you cannot remember a time when you acted at the regeneration level, consider how it might feel to do so.

_____

_____

_____

What would it be like to look at the world with a greater awareness of the present and greater openness to new information?

_____

_____

_____

What do you think would change in your approach to challenges and in your relationships?

_____

_____

_____

What prevents you from acting at the higher levels more often? What could you do about it?

_____

_____

_____

REGENERATION OF A RELATIONSHIP

When we are truly committed to creating a new result, we change. The quality of our attention shifts. Eventually, we begin to pay attention to how we pay attention. When we change how we observe the world, we change our relationship with the world. In that new relationship we can lead from the future as it emerges.

There is a story about a mother and child that I often present to executives to illustrate self-change and regeneration in a relationship. At first it seems distant and unconnected to the world of work. Yet it is deeply connected and worthy of close examination.

The case, which comes from the work of Terry Warner (2001, pp. 1–4), describes an eight-year-old girl who has no interest in doing her homework. Her mother insists that she complete her homework, and spends hours working with her. The child complains. The mother tries to be cheerful but becomes increasingly irritated. The mother states, "The trouble with Erin is especially frustrating because for years I have given her my best efforts."

The mother then describes the self-discipline she has had to exercise not to compare Erin with her sister, who is highly motivated and a good student. The mother frequently gives Erin warm hugs, assuring the child that she is loved. She describes drilling Erin with flash cards and Erin's seemingly perverse efforts to frustrate the effort by knowingly giving wrong answers. She says that she feels as if she has been "kicked in the teeth" and feels helpless to change her daughter.

Had I been this woman's friend or consultant, I would have assured her that this kind of frustration is universal. Her challenges are no different from those faced by a basketball coach who cannot get his players to excel, a sales manager who cannot get her salesforce to accept a new technique, or the executives at GM who could not turn around the Fremont plant. Indeed, there are striking connections.

In the face of failure, reaching for help is often a critical move. Erin's mother did just that. She attended a self-help workshop run by Warner, where he encouraged her to look more deeply into herself. This process had considerable impact. She went through a personal change that also altered how she saw the world. As she reflected on her relationship with Erin, she noted considerable self-deception and realized that she was implicitly communicating her own negative feelings. "I was outwardly encouraging, but inwardly I mistrusted her," the mother said. "[Erin] felt that message from me."

With her new and more complex worldview, the mother took on a higher level of concern for her daughter: "I cried when I realized the price she had to pay for my inability to love her without reservation."

With a new vision for the relationship, Erin's mother stopped micromanaging the relationship and began modeling the importance of self-discipline, encouraging Erin to come to her for help when she was ready. After some weeks, the little girl began to perform well in school.

Erin's mother went on to report a moment that demonstrated how much the relationship had changed.

I pulled her up on my lap . . . and I had this overwhelming feeling of love . . . that just seemed to flow between us. I hugged her tightly, and told her how much I loved her. I realized that, for the very first time in eight years, I was expressing true love for her. . . . It was as if I was holding a new baby for the first time. Tears were streaming down, and she looked at me and said, "Are you crying because you love me, Mommy?" I nodded. She whispered, "Mommy, I want to stay with you forever."

Think About It

- What connections do you see between Erin's mother's frustrations and the challenges faced by the basketball coach who cannot get his players to excel, the sales manager who cannot get her team to accept a new technique, or the GM executives who could not turn around the Fremont plant?

  _____

  _____

  _____

- What similar frustrations have you experienced? What did you do to address those challenges? How successful were you?

  _____

  _____

  _____

THE TRANSFORMATIONAL PROCESS

The story of Erin and her mother is relevant to executives because it is about a change agent who believes her motives are pure as she tries to change a person who occupies a lower place in the hierarchy.

Consider these important details: The change agent (the mother) defines a problem—the unwillingness of an eight-year-old to study. She describes the purity of her own motives, the logic of her strategy, the resistance in the change target (Erin), and her frustration. These are behaviors common to the normal change agent.

The mother, like the GM executives, is sure that the problem does not lie within. It is her daughter who needs to be fixed. That is the normal pattern.

Then the mother finds herself in a situation where she is able to lower her defenses and examine her motives, her thought processes, and her behaviors. She discovers that she has been deceiving herself. Because she believed her motives to be pure, she could not recognize that her strategies for changing Erin were actually selfish. When we believe our motives are pure, it is difficult for us to understand how our actions might be destroying a relationship we need to enrich. It is also hard to believe that responsibility for the problem lies anywhere but with the other people.

When the change agent (the mother) gains a new, more self-reflective vision, her behaviors change. These new behaviors send a new message. The change target (Erin) has to pay attention to make sense of the new patterns. She becomes aware that she is no longer being judged and objectified as a problem. In the warmth and safety of her mother's love, she finds increased confidence and feels safe to experiment with new behaviors of her own.

To change, Erin's mother had to transcend a script that she carried in her head. Such change is a transformation that results in new understanding and new capacity. When we gain new understanding and capacity, we can live in the present moment in a more adaptive way. We do not have to be fearful and rigid because we can blend our intention with the unfolding future.

Self-change almost always brings increased clarity of purpose, increased integrity, increased concern for others, and greater awareness of and openness to the potential that surrounds us. In this case the mother became more committed to the real growth of her child. She became less self-deceptive and more authentic. She was filled with genuine love. She became aware of new realities and possibilities.

Think About It

- Have you ever experienced a changed relationship, when another person began to show you genuine concern, or have you ever made this change toward someone else? What happened?

_____

_____

_____

- Can you recall a time when you were having difficulty getting someone to change his or her behavior?

_____

_____

_____

What messages were you sending?

_____

_____

_____

How did your own certainty that you were right affect the person's willingness to change?

_____

_____

_____

If you were in the same situation again, what might you do differently?

_____

_____

_____

THE CONNECTIONS

A central message of this field guide is that assumptions matter. From the Buddha we learn: "What we are today comes from our thoughts of yesterday, and our present thoughts build our life of tomorrow: our life is the creation of our mind."

Consider again the assumptions guiding the behavior of the GM executives at the failed GM plant in Fremont. The executives had learned from their observations of yesterday. They might, for example, have introduced a new technique only to see a union group immediately discredit it. The union's actions would have reconfirmed the executives' beliefs that they were at war with the unions.

Naturally, they would have negative feelings toward the people who had treated them in this way

The executives' experience verified their belief that they lived in a world of conflict. This understanding of the present led them to imagine a future that looked the same as the world from which they had drawn their assumptions. Thus, they continued to act on their negative feelings—which could be felt by the employees just as Erin could perceive her mother's negative thoughts and feelings. As a result, the union members acted just as Erin did. They refused to cooperate and sometimes tried to sabotage the executives' efforts, again confirming to the executives that their view of the world was correct. Because they were unable to examine their own assumptions and change themselves, they could not change the people they desired to change; instead, they found fault with them.

By doing this, the executives became carriers of the disease they were trying to eradicate. The conflict and distrust they detested were embodied in their core assumptions and spread by their every action. Because they could not make the deep personal change necessary to make deep change in their organization's culture, they were caught in a vicious cycle that led to hopelessness and failure.

But failure is never inevitable. As the eventual success of the Fremont plant demonstrated, organizational growth and success come from alternative perspectives. The Toyota executives were confident that by working with the Fremont plant's employees they could produce a transformation. Managers and employees would exist in a cooperative relationship built on trust; the result would be personal and organizational transformation.

Think About It

- Have you ever been part of an organization that failed?

_____

_____

_____

How much of that failure was the result of leaders acting on assumptions based on their experience?

_____

_____

_____

Who did the leaders believe was at fault for the failure?

_____

_____

_____

What might have happened if the leaders had examined their normal assumptions and changed themselves first?

_____

_____

_____

DENIAL

I used the story of Erin and her mother as an analogy for thinking about leadership in an organization. I asked you to look for commonalities between the two types of relationships. This may have been difficult. In the family, we accept the possibility of intimacy and love, particularly between mother and child. No one could expect a GM executive to state, "I cried when I realized the price my people had to pay because of my inability to love them without reservation."

According to the normal assumption set, work is not a place for love. It is a place of self-interested, transactional exchange. It is a place where people pretend to cooperate while pursuing resources for themselves. At GM, an executive had to be tough to avoid being exploited by superiors, peers, and subordinates. This assumption of competition is central in most organizations. It is central in most personal relationships. It was central in how Erin's mother initially related to Erin. For a long time it was difficult for the mother to see any other way.

I am reminded of an executive who told me he understood the principles I was teaching. He and his wife used them in their family. When he or his wife wanted to change the behavior of their teenager, they learned to first look at themselves. They practiced self-mastery and closed their own integrity gaps. The results were impressive. Yet, he told me, "I cannot imagine how to bring these same principles into my professional setting." His assumptions about work were determining the nature of his relationships at work.

SOFT IS HARD

When I suggest that assumptions of excellence and deep change apply in all systems, from families to corporations, my students get uneasy. They cannot readily see how an approach that values self-reflection, trust, and selflessness could succeed in an organizational setting. Sometimes they even respond with derisive statements like, "I do not buy that 'soft' crap."

This might sound like a statement of strength; it is actually a statement of weakness and fear. It means that doing the work of deep change is too "hard." We want to be oblivious to the harm caused by our efforts to force change on others. We may sense that we are living in damaged, conditional relationships, but we fear knowing more because the truth would require us to change.

The people who are not interested in that "soft crap" are the ones who often design changes that fail and then blame the failure on a culture that would not change. But changing a culture is the leader's responsibility, and if culture does not change the leader has failed.

This chapter challenges a widely held assumption: that cultural change is something conceived and imposed by people of authority. In acting on this assumption, people seek to impose change on others that they are unwilling to make themselves. But any attempt to change culture must begin with self-change. As CEO Andrea Jung suggests, when we change ourselves we suddenly see both ourselves and the people around us in a new light. We see how our own defenses have kept us from recognizing our own role in causing the problems we wish to solve. When we make deep change at the personal level, we begin to see the potential in the people around us, even those whom we had written off, and we see in them the power to unleash the full potential of the organization.

Personal Reflection and Application

REFLECT

While the chapter is fresh in your mind, quickly write down the 4 to 6 points, concepts, or ideas that stand out for you the most.

WATCH THE FILM: *THE KING'S SPEECH*

In this film, the Duke of York, second son of the King of England, has a serious problem: he stutters. This may sound like a personal matter, but it is not. It is a problem for the Empire. Like anyone with a visible position in a large organization, he must represent his organization by speaking in public. The prince was not born with a stutter. It was a learned characteristic that had become part of his identity. To solve the problem, the prince has to change the assumptions he has made about himself. He has to change his identity. After many others try unsuccessfully to help the prince, a speech therapist named Lionel Logue leads him through the deep change process. We might do well to study what this man did.

Questions to Consider

1. What does the prince believe about his ability to change? In what ways is he like Norma Rae?

   _____

   _____

   _____

2. The first person we see trying to help the prince is the doctor who asks him to speak with marbles in his mouth.

   _____

   _____

   _____

   - How much confidence do you have in the doctor? Why?

   _____

   _____

   _____

- In terms of bringing change, what assumptions does the doctor make?

_____

_____

_____

- How are his assumptions limiting his effectiveness?

_____

_____

_____

3. When Lionel meets Elizabeth, he indicates he can cure anyone who wants to be healed. Why is Lionel so confident? Where does his confidence come from?

_____

_____

_____

4. Lionel indicates that for his method to work there must be absolute trust and total equality within his consultation room.

_____

_____

_____

- How are these assumptions different from the assumptions made by others? Why are they necessary?

_____

_____

_____

- In terms of their ability to bring change, how would you compare Lionel with the doctor?

_____

_____

_____

5. King George V has his own approach to solving his son's problem.

   _____

   _____

   _____

   - What is his theory of change? How effective is it?

     _____

     _____

     _____

   - What assumptions would you have him change to be more effective?

     _____

     _____

     _____

6. Lionel asks if the prince was born right-handed and learns that he was not. He also asks other questions that suggest deep insight into the prince's life patterns. Why does Lionel pay attention to these patterns when no one else has?

   _____

   _____

   _____

7. Lionel tells his wife that he has a client who is full of fear. She suggests that all of his clients are. Lionel indicates that this one could be great. His wife responds that perhaps the man does not want to be great. Do you agree with Lionel's wife? Why or why not? How does this issue apply to you?

   _____

   _____

   _____

8. When the prince confronts Lionel about his not having a medical degree, Lionel replies that his qualification is success and his success comes from experience. How do you respond to this? Why does it matter to the prince that Lionel does not have a degree?

_____

_____

_____

9. After Lionel offends the prince by sitting in the royal chair, they argue about the value of the trappings of hierarchy. Lionel asks why he should listen to the prince. The prince says that he has a right to be heard "as a man. *I have a voice.*" Lionel assures him that he does and that the prince is the bravest man he knows.

_____

_____

_____

• Why does Lionel think the prince is brave?

_____

_____

_____

• What happened in this exchange? How does the moment link to what happened previously?

_____

_____

_____

10. What do you see as the most common characteristics of Lionel and the characters in the earlier films: Reuben, Norma, and Billy Beane? What do those characteristics tell you about becoming a transformational mentor?

_____

_____

_____

11. List the key insights you gained from the film about the power of self-change and briefly describe some life experiences that you associate with these insights.

_____

_____

_____

MAKE A JOURNAL ENTRY

Read the following statements. Check the 2 or 3 that resonate most with you.

___1. Few people ever clearly see the incongruity of asking for deep change in others while failing to commit to deep self-change.

___2. Organizations are full of potential that can be released through constant, positive, proactive change.

___3. People with long experience sometimes cannot "look at the business with fresh eyes."

___4. "I've had to reinvent myself every year."

___5. Shuffling the boxes on the organizational chart looks like change but ignores the fact that, in many cases, the real problem is in the culture.

___6. Holding onto normal assumptions will keep change efforts from succeeding, no matter how many resources we invest.

___7. To create an innovative result, we must become fully aware of the present.

___8. Self-change almost always brings increased clarity of purpose, increased integrity, increased concern for others, and greater awareness of and openness to the potential that surrounds us.

___9. Those of us who are inclined to be in charge and to impose change on others are often the most resistant to self-understanding.

___10. When we make deep change at the personal level, we embody deep change and we begin to see the potential in the people around us.

Now circle the number of the single statement you most resonate with. List some life experiences that you associate with that statement. Then write a paragraph that expresses the importance of one of those life experiences.

Life experiences:

_____

_____

_____

Paragraph:

_____

_____

_____

WRITE A MEMO

Based on your insights, your responses to the questions about the film, and your journal entry, write a short note to someone you know. Help the person understand the essence of what you have learned in this chapter.

_____

_____

_____

_____

APPLY THE LEARNING

What are one or two actions you will take from what you have learned in this chapter to continue your journey toward mastery of the deep change process?

_____

_____

_____

_____

CHAPTER FOUR

PERSONAL CHANGE AND POSITIVE ORGANIZING

IN THIS CHAPTER

- We can choose to see ourselves as static or dynamic.
- Moments of great stress can sometimes teach us to look at the world with new assumptions.
- The assumptions of positive organizing can help us build more productive organizations.

Buckminster Fuller once made an interesting claim: "I live on Earth at present, and I don't know what I am. I know that I am not a category. I am not a thing—a noun. I seem to be a verb, an evolutionary process—an integral function of the universe."

This statement suggests a dynamic view of the self. The world is always changing and we must adapt. Yet we often regard ourselves as a noun, not a verb. The notion of regarding self as a verb suggests that we accept the idea that we must continually adapt.

An entrepreneur who went bankrupt described the experience as follows: "I could no longer say that I 'was' my job, because I had none. I couldn't rely on my wealth to create a sense of worth and identity, for I had no money and loads of debt. I could not look to social standing, for a failed entrepreneur has no social standing. And the failure of my love relationship a month earlier ensured that

I could not find myself through the love of another. I had nothing, therefore I was nothing. And I had died" (Youngblood, 1997, p. 208).

This kind of failure can drop us into a world of personal chaos. Yet it can also serve as a period of great learning and development. When our world turns upside down, we are forced to search out new possibilities and engage in new experiences.

Chaos tends to take us to our root: our core values and our truest desires. We gain the capacity to work our way out of chaos as we clarify our values. Clarifying our values means specifying our most essential self. Through the process, we come to know what about ourselves we will not change. We become more internally driven, more courageous and authentic. This gives us the stability necessary to be adaptive and learn our way through the change process.

THE DEATH AND REBIRTH OF OUR EGO

Here, the failed entrepreneur describes what came out of the trauma caused by the bankruptcy:

> Until that point, I had lived my life through the eyes of other people. I had defined myself through object-reference—my sense of identity and my feelings of self-worth were tied directly to the outer circumstances of my life—all of these external references were stripped away. When I looked in the mirror, I did not know who I was. For me, the ego-death and subsequent "rebirth" was a wonderfully and powerfully transformative event. I experienced a sort of "awakening" in which I realized in a flash of insight that "I" was not my ego or the external trappings of my life. "I" was still all that [it] had ever been, my true self. Nothing that was real and certain had changed, just superficial aspects of my environment (Youngblood, 1997, p. 208).

The entrepreneur describes his loss of identity, or *ego-death*, as transformative. He goes on to make several important points about the process:

- In the past, he was externally directed. He organized himself according to what he thought other people would think of him.
- He now recognized that when externalities were swept away, he did not know who he was.

- The "death" of the old identity was followed by a transformative "rebirth."
- His rebirth came of the realization that his most essential self was not based on external reinforcements.
- He learned that failure is not permanent if we are in a truly adaptive state.
- He discovered that he did not have to orient his identity around his fears.

Think About It

- Have you experienced the process of ego-death or witnessed the process in someone else?

  _____

  _____

  _____

- What is your most important insight about ego-death?

  _____

  _____

  _____

- What is your most important insight about the rebirth of the ego?

  _____

  _____

  _____

TURNING POINTS

Research suggests that many of us experience such transformation and redirection. We experience changes that serve as the turning points or episodes when we take a new view of self, experience a change in identity, or find new meaning in life. Research suggests the following about turning points (Wethington, 2003).

- *They are memorable.* Turning points are manifest not in life events that reaffirm how we see ourselves, but in out-of-the-ordinary events that give rise to revelatory insights, reevaluations of a position, or the emergence of a new capability. They are often associated with the sense of becoming a new or renewed person.

- *They are challenging.* The more stressful an event, the more likely it will become a turning point.
- *They are often positive.* Many turning points are triggered by positive events, such as mastering a life challenge, reaching an important milestone, or taking on a new role, such as that of a spouse, a parent, or a leader. They may result from succeeding at a challenge or task or receiving meaningful appreciation, or from prayer, meditation, fasting, or a significant religious experience.
- *They can be negative events.* Perceptions of growth and increased capacity can also come from setbacks such as the one experienced by the entrepreneur. When faced with a negative situation, we may eventually learn to master a problem, discover what is really important to us, gain confidence, learn we can withstand stress, or gain a greater self-understanding. Those who have experienced turning points in this context often speak in terms of lessons learned. They report achieving higher self-esteem, stronger relationships, greater recognition from others, or better health.

PROCESSING NEGATIVE EVENTS

Although we are sometimes able to talk about significant emotional events shortly after they happen, some traumas get buried (Niederhoffer and Pennebaker, 2002). For example, we can be reluctant to speak of events like abuse, rape, and personal failure that give rise to negative emotions like embarrassment, shame, and fear.

Traumas like the one experienced by the failed entrepreneur often lead to a disruption of core identity. We feel disoriented because the world no longer seems predictable. The mind keeps returning to the event, trying to construct a meaningful story that restores a sense of control and a feeling of being in sync with the core self.

Niederhoffer and Pennebaker (2002) suggest that disclosing the event in written or verbal form may increase our ability to understand what happened and integrate the experience into our meaning system. The process of constructing the story is important because it creates a sense of causality, and this allows us to accept the event intellectually. Sharing is particularly important because it can increase social integration. When we keep a trauma secret we may behave in guarded ways that detach us from our social networks, which are a venue for growth where we can experiment and change. Writing or talking about the trauma alters how we think about it. It allows us to shift away from the negative and move toward exploration. As we redefine the meaning of the event, as we construct its story, we regain a sense of predictability and control. We may feel a sense of resolution so that we can let the event recede into the past.

Think About It

- Have you ever experienced a turning point, either professionally or personally?

  _____

  _____

  _____

- What led up to the experience?

  _____

  _____

  _____

- What was your most important takeaway?

  _____

  _____

  _____

DEEP CHANGE AND GENERATIVE CAPACITY

I once gave a talk about deep change to a group of venture capitalists and CEOs of start-up firms. A woman I will call Anna came up to tell me her own story of self-change. She began with a declaration: "I have a very unique skill. I create companies. I bring people together, and out of nothing, I make something. That is what I do." Although she said this with enormous confidence, it was not a statement of hubris. Rather, she spoke with a sense of wonder. It was as if she was being vitalized by this recognition of her own ability.

I was impressed. Imagine being confident that you can enter new situations and bring people together in such a way that a new company emerges. This is adaptive confidence—the belief in one's capacity to lead deep change. I asked her how she had acquired this capacity.

"I went through a terrible life crisis," she said. "I was without work. I hungered to get back into my comfort zone. So I took a job just like the one I was in before. After three months, I realized that I had made a mistake. So I decided to leave my job and live without an income. Previously I thought people loved me because I made money. I discovered that they loved me because of who I am. I discovered I could do things I did not know I could do. I gained a new identity and a higher level of confidence in myself. I could see in new ways and I was not afraid to try new things."

Anna experienced a change in identity. Like the failed entrepreneur, she had been defining herself in terms of external incentives. Such identity assumptions lead us to conclude that we must achieve to be loved. Also like the entrepreneur, her experience of failure allowed her to transcend this widely held assumption and other normal assumptions, giving her sure knowledge that she could make deep change, and thus, that others could also make deep change.

Turning points cause us to see ourselves differently. Whether they result from positive or negative events, they capture our attention and invite a new definition of self. When this happens, we, like Anna, discover two things for sure: we know that we can change, and thus we know that others can change too. This knowledge is essential to people who seek to lead deep change. As we use self-reflection to grow and become more positive and more influential, we acquire the desire to change our external context, a trait sometimes called *developmental readiness* (Avolio and Hannah, 2008). This may create a virtuous cycle of initiative and learning. Living in this cycle we become empowered and empowering to others.

Think About It

- Have you ever felt the kind of adaptive confidence claimed by Anna?

_____

_____

_____

- Where does such confidence originate?

_____

_____

_____

- What would lead you to such confidence?

_____

_____

_____

TWO REALITIES

As mentioned in earlier chapters, normal assumptions lead us to see as others do. We think the same things, we do the same things, and we get similar results. But the assumptions associated with excellence lead us to see, think, and act differently. Each set of assumptions leads to a different reality.

Table 4.1 shows two different approaches to organizing human behavior that lead us to see two different realities. The list on the left contains the assumptions of normal organizing. The list on the right contains the assumptions associated with excellence. I call this second process *positive organizing*.

TABLE 4.1 TWO REALITIES

Assumptions of Normal Organizing	Assumptions of Positive Organizing
People	People
. . . pursue their self-interest.	. . . sacrifice for the common good.
. . . pursue external rewards.	. . . pursue intrinsic satisfaction.
. . . live in assumptions of exchange.	. . . live in assumptions of contribution.
. . . minimize personal costs.	. . . go beyond expectations.
. . . assume hierarchy.	. . . assume equality.
. . . see constraints.	. . . envision possibilities.
. . . comply with expectations.	. . . empower themselves.
. . . prefer the status quo.	. . . initiate change.
. . . engage in conflict.	. . . build trust.
. . . become alienated.	. . . live in high-quality connections.
. . . fail to learn.	. . . experiment and discover.
. . . compete for scarce resources.	. . . expand the resource pool.

The items in the left-hand column describe normal behaviors that result from normal assumptions. The items in the right-hand column suggest what people and organizations are like when they are performing very well. They reflect the findings from two new fields: positive psychology and positive organizational scholarship. Researchers in these fields ask, "What are things like when they are at their best?"

As we saw in earlier chapters, normal assumptions usually lead to entropy and slow death. In organizations, when people in authority make normal assumptions they explicitly or implicitly communicate those assumptions. Others, already predisposed to these normal assumptions, begin to enact them. The assumptions become more deeply etched in the people and the culture. The organization then begins to follow a more negative trajectory.

Many people believe that the items in the right-hand column represent unrealistic aspirations. In contrast, transformational leaders embrace the items on the right. They see possibilities, communicate high expectations, and support people in moving from the left to the right. The items on the right are realistic, they just occur more rarely than the items on the left.

Think About It

Take another look at the two approaches to organizing in Table 4.1 and consider these questions:

- Have you ever known someone who seemed to look at things from the assumptions of positive organizing? What kind of energy did that person project? What kinds of results did that person achieve?

  _____

  _____

  _____

- Thinking back to the Buckminster Fuller quote at the start of the chapter about seeing self as a noun or a verb, what might it have to do with each of the two lists of assumptions?

  _____

  _____

  _____

- Which of the two columns most closely describes your own assumptions? Why do you think that is so?

  ___ Assumptions of normal organizing

  ___ Assumptions of positive organizing

SUCCESS SCRIPTS

A script is a text that informs someone of what they are to say. Just as actors do onstage, we follow scripts in our daily lives. Our scripts come from our past experiences, and we are rarely conscious of them. For example, many of us continue to relate to our parents and siblings as we did when we were growing up.

Gretchen Spreitzer, a professor at the University of Michigan, and I analyzed the assumptions professionals make about their personal and professional success (Quinn and Spreitzer, 1991). When we analyzed the commonalities in their profiles, we found that people tended to hold one of four different sets of assumptions about the kinds of behaviors that would make them successful.

We wrote of these as success myths. We used the word myth not to suggest illusion, but to describe how people carry stories, theories, or assumptions that organize their lives. Here, we often refer to them as *success scripts*. While success scripts may structure behavior, they do not necessarily assure success; as we will see, they may even lead to negative conditions such as low life satisfaction.

The first two scripts tend to be held by people we classified as *individual contributors*, people who work alone and do not supervise others. The second two tend to be held by people with leadership responsibilities. Here are the four scripts.

The Script of Responsive Service

I am at my best when given an assignment that allows me to serve others. I love work that matches my ideals. I minimize time spent planning, pay little attention to structure, and avoid intensity (stress) so that I can engage in action. I learn by reflecting on this action. I am flexible and open and I look for intuitive insights. When the task is completed, I am satisfied because my work has made the world a better place. I then move on, looking for a new opportunity to serve.

Eight percent of the people in our study followed this script. They were the youngest group, idealistic, with good health habits and a low tolerance for task variety. Most of them were not satisfied with their work, their pay, or their relationships with coworkers or their supervisor. Although these young people were idealistic, they seemed to be underutilized and undervalued by the organization.

The Script of Independent Task Pursuit

I am at my best when I am given an assignment that is specific. I organize in a careful, analytical way. I define clear objectives and make detailed timetables. I work alone, making an intense individual effort with no regard for feedback. I feel fulfilled when I receive approval after the task is complete. I stay connected to the activity or product.

Twenty-eight percent of the people in our study followed this script. They tended to be less educated, with a lower locus of control, lower tolerance for change and stress, lower life satisfaction, and lower job involvement. Although they valued independence highly, they tended to be disempowered and dependent on others.

The Script of Intense Achievement

I am at my best when I am challenged to demonstrate my ability and have the opportunity to obtain appropriate rewards. I take charge of groups to provide vision and direction. I am intensely action-focused, overcoming barriers and emphasizing goal achievement. I feel fulfilled when I reach my goals and others recognize my accomplishments. I then turn things over to another.

Forty-six percent of the respondents followed this script. They were seen as charismatic by their subordinates. They had a high tolerance for social stimulation, task variety, change, and stress. They reported high work satisfaction, and were satisfied with their supervisors and their promotions. These people are leaders who love to be challenged, rewarded, and recognized. They are ready to take charge and get results. They strive to meet the normal expectations of good leadership.

The Script of Collective Fulfillment

I am at my best when I can do something that fits my values. I am not motivated by rewards; I am purpose-driven. I serve others. I bring together a collective and help them develop and embrace a unique vision. I nurture commitment and cohesion by expanding participation and building trust. I stay open to feedback and new alternatives. I feel fulfilled when the group begins to mature. I value the relationships and products of the community and I stay connected to it.

Eighteen percent of the study participants fit this script. They were the oldest group. They had high satisfaction with life, pay, and coworkers. Other people did not rate them as charismatic as the preceding group. Although they were results-centered, they did not seek external approval; instead, they were internally directed. They were driven by purpose but oriented to people, eliciting vision from the people around them and building cohesive effort. They did not seem to be seeking external rewards but internal satisfaction. They were externally open, able to move forward while learning and adapting in real time.

Think About It
• Which of the four success scripts do you think best describes you? Why do you think that is so?

____ Script of responsive service

____ Script of independent task pursuit

____ Script of intense achievement

____ Script of collective fulfillment

- Does another one of the scripts describe the kind of outlook you would like to have? Which one? What is it about that script that you find appealing?

  _____

  _____

  _____

- What could you do to become more like the people who follow the script that you would prefer to follow?

  _____

  _____

  _____

CHANGING THE SCRIPT

It may be that these scripts follow a developmental pattern. Deep change is about acquiring new assumptions. For someone to shift from the assumptions of independent task pursuit to the script of intense achievement or from the script of intense achievement to the script of collective fulfillment would be a deep change. Here are three examples.

Becoming a Manager

An engineer I will call Luis, who had graduated from a five-year program in four years, had been successful at the job he had taken after graduation. A technically competent, innovative, and action-oriented person, he was promoted several times. The last promotion, however, placed him in a supervisory position. For the first time in his career, he received serious negative feedback from his supervisors. His ideas and proposals were regularly rejected, and he was passed over for another promotion. He worried that he had reached his "level of incompetence" but he refused to give up.

Luis faced a common problem. When he became a supervisor, he found that his technical models and hard-edged strategies were no longer working. He felt that the kinds of personal participation and political involvement required of him were antithetical to everything he believed. Finally, a critical incident occurred. Like many critical incidents in the deep change process, it seems trivial, but it caused him to reevaluate his perspective.

Several times, Luis's boss had commented that she was very impressed with one of his subordinates because no matter how early she herself arrived at work, this man's car was always in the parking lot. When Luis spoke to his subordinate, the man explained, "I have four teenagers who wake up at dawn. The mornings at my house are chaotic, so I come in early. I read the paper, have some coffee, and then start work at eight."

At first, Luis was furious that his subordinate should be given such high praise for behaviors that had nothing to do with his commitment to the organization. Then he began to laugh. He later said, "From that point forward, everything started to change." He came to appreciate the fact that perception, or what he called political reality, is as important—and real—as technical reality. At that moment, his assumptions were transformed and his thinking processes became more complex.

"During those terrible years," he explained, "I occasionally thought I had reached my level of incompetence, but I refused to give up. The frustration and pain turned out to be positive things because they forced me to consider alternative perspectives. I eventually learned that there were other realities besides the technical reality.

"At higher levels, what matters is how people see the world, and everyone sees it a little differently. Things change more rapidly. You are no longer buffered from the outside world. Challenges are more complex, and it takes longer to get people onboard. I decided I had to be a lot more receptive and a lot more patient. It was an enormous adjustment, but finally things started to change. I think I became a much better manager."

Luis underwent a classic personal transformation. He transcended the success script of independent task pursuit and the mindset of the technician. He had changed how he viewed himself and his world. It was a deep change—not unlike a religious conversion.

He began to see the organization in a more dynamic way. He also began to more fully understand that the organization was not only a technical system but also a political system and a moral system. He became more appreciative of the fact that many people were living the script of intense achievement. In the meantime, he adapted a number of new behaviors that reflected the script of collective fulfillment.

Although he now focused more on nontechnical realities, he did not lose his technical capacity. Instead, Luis became a more effective version of his former self. After his transformation, he understood the world better and operated in it with greater effectiveness.

The Transformation of a Manager

Just as Luis moved beyond his script of independent task pursuit, it is possible to move out of the script of intense achievement. Consider a case from Csikszentmihalyi (1997). The case describes Keith, a manager who worked seventy hours a week, neglecting his family and his own personal growth and hoarding credit for his accomplishments, in an attempt to impress his superiors and win a promotion. Nevertheless, he was still passed over.

"Finally Keith resigned himself to having reached the ceiling of his career, and decided to find his rewards elsewhere. He spent more time with the family, took up a hobby, became involved in community activities. Because he was no longer struggling so hard, his behavior on the job became more relaxed, less selfish, and more objective. In fact, he began to act more like a leader whose personal agenda takes second place to the well-being of the company" (pp. 113–114). Keith's boss was finally impressed, and he received his promotion.

Keith's shift was a personal process of deep change. As he made the change, he became a more effective version of himself. After moving from the script of intense achievement to the script of collective fulfillment, Keith was prepared to be a transformational leader.

The Transformation of a CEO

People operating in the script of intense achievement may move up many levels. They may even reach the top. But ascending to a position of authority does not make someone a fully effective change agent.

I think of a well-known CEO, a brilliant man with a thirst for action and achievement whom I will call Marty. During his first five years as CEO, Marty globalized his company and drove it to impressive levels of profit. Almost everyone considered him to be a first-rate leader. He was a success. Then his story took a curious turn.

As Marty entered his sixth year as CEO, things grew more difficult. He seemed to have driven the system as far as he could drive it. As he wrestled with his challenges, he also began to talk about the need for values and the commitment to values. He wanted to develop something he called a *high-performance culture*, one that valued task completion while also valuing high-quality human relationships.

Marty was making a deep change. He was shifting from one success script to another. He had been on the journey of intense achievement, and in the process, he discovered that he himself had to grow if his company was to grow.

It is interesting that, as Marty tried to build the new culture, he often pointed out that he was not interested in being "warm and fuzzy." He remained very committed to achievement and accountability as he built a culture of respect, trust, collaboration, experimentation, and learning. What brought him to this conclusion? He had made a personal discovery. In a personal conversation, he told me:

> Sooner or later, every leader comes to understand how little power he or she really has. As we became more complex and the environment more intense, it became impossible to get things done through the force of leadership. Everything in my mind had always been so clear and logical. I felt [that] if we just did what we knew how to do every day, this thing [would] work. I had this grand scheme and grand design and grand vision and I thought I could articulate it and get people lined up. It did not happen. I think that I had to come to grips with the fact that it is not enough for me to be committed, to have a plan and understand where we are going. I realized I had to get everyone engaged and committed.

The script of intense achievement assumes that a focused personality with transactional skills can make things happen. This is frequently true. But like all normal scripts, the script of intense achievement eventually reaches the limit of its effectiveness. Marty, a brilliant thinker and shrewd student of management, discovered that limit: "Sooner or later, every leader comes to understand how little power he or she really has." How could he say such a thing? He was the CEO. He had all the formal authority one could ever hope to have. Yet it was not enough. In a highly complex and dynamic environment, one mind, even a brilliant mind, is not enough. In order to accomplish the great goals he had set for his company, Marty needed to move to the next script. He began moving toward the script of collective fulfillment. Only by developing a culture of engaged relationships could he build a great company. To continue growing, the company needed to become a place of positive organizing.

Just as the engineer who becomes a more effective manager still keeps his technical understanding, the leader who embraces the script of collective fulfillment and the assumptions of positive organizing continues to understand the dynamics of normal reality. Because this leader can now see multiple realities, however, his or her ability to detect, understand, and solve problems is greater than it was before. By the same token, such a leader will recognize human potential and see opportunities where others do not. The leader who has embraced positive reality to follow the script of collective fulfillment is thus able to bring growth where transactional leaders have already given up in frustration.

Think About It

- What do these three stories have in common? In what ways do they reveal how the script of intense achievement can limit our understanding?

  _____

  _____

  _____

  Think of a leader you have known who followed the script of intense achievement and one who followed the script of collective fulfillment. Write a few words that describe the typical behavior of each leader.

  Leader who followed the script of intense achievement:

  _____

  _____

  _____

  _____

  Leader who followed the script of collective fulfillment:

_____

_____

_____

_____

- How did the behaviors of these leaders differ?

_____

_____

_____

PERSONAL CHANGE AND POSITIVE ORGANIZING

At the start of the chapter I quoted Buckminster Fuller: "I live on Earth at present, and I don't know what I am. I know that I am not a category. I am not a thing—a noun. I seem to be a verb, an evolutionary process—an integral function of the universe."

The statement suggests that we live in a universe of constant change, and there is a need for continual adaptation. The self must be continually evolving. As we experience the turning points of life, we do evolve. As we evolve, we gain new understanding and capacity. First, we learn how to be successful and achieve recognition. The challenge is then to move on. We must learn how to be excellent, how to bring about the realization of the collective good through positive organizing.

Personal Reflection and Application

REFLECT

While the chapter is fresh in your mind, quickly write down the 4 to 6 points, concepts, or ideas that stand out for you the most.

WATCH THE FILM: *THE DEVIL WEARS PRADA*

This film follows the experiences of Andrea, a young woman who is hired at *Runway*, a top fashion magazine, where the culture is dominated by assumptions of control, hierarchy, exchange, and competition. It is a culture in which managers and employees constantly criticize each other's clothing, weight, and job performance. After several terrible months on the job, Andrea experiences a turning point, and she is surprised to discover that her boss, Miranda, who treated her so poorly, ultimately comes to hold her in high regard. The film has much to teach us about organizations and personal change.

Questions to Consider

1. Andrea is a novice entering her first professional job setting.

   • What are some of the initial indicators that she has entered a culture dominated by the desire for external recognition?

   _____

   _____

   _____

   _____

   • What are some of her first small acts of surrender to this culture?

   _____

   _____

   _____

   _____

2. When the group is choosing belts, Andrea laughs and draws the ire of Miranda, who zeroes in on the color of Andrea's sweater. Miranda does a brilliant analysis of how the industry works to make the point that Andrea's choice of sweater was determined in that very room.

- What does this conversation tell you about Miranda?

_____

_____

_____

_____

- What are Miranda's strengths?

_____

_____

_____

_____

3. Miranda often "gets to" Andrea, but Andrea seems to feel particularly pained when Miranda says that she is disappointed with Andrea's performance.
   - Why does this particular statement hurt Andrea so much?

_____

_____

_____

_____

   - What can we learn about Andrea's motivations from her reaction?

_____

_____

_____

_____

4. When Andrea is staggering under the pressure of the job, she goes to Nigel for advice. Instead of comforting her, he points out the greatness of the organization, tells Andrea she is not really committed, and says that she needs to "wake up."

- Is there greatness in the organization? What is it?

_____

_____

_____

_____

- What is he really telling her to do?

_____

_____

_____

_____

- What happens because of his suggestions?

_____

_____

_____

_____

5. Miranda challenged Andrea by giving her a nearly impossible task: find an advance copy of the Harry Potter book for her children.

- Why did Miranda give Andrea this task, which had nothing to do with her job?

_____

_____

_____

_____

- How did Andrea handle it?

_____

_____

_____

_____

- How did Andrea's performance impact their relationship?

  _____

  _____

  _____

  _____

6. When someone's behavior changes, people around them often suggest that the person's values have changed. Andrea's boyfriend, accusing her of becoming a "Runway Girl," says, "The person whose calls you always take, that is the relationship you are in." When another friend says that she does not understand the person Andrea has become, Andrea responds, "I did not have a choice."

   - What does Andrea mean?

     _____

     _____

     _____

     _____

   - What similarities do you see between Andrea's statement and the kinds of values the entrepreneur mentioned in this chapter held before his bankruptcy?

     _____

     _____

     _____

     _____

   - When have you felt that you were in a difficult, negative situation but that you "didn't have a choice?"

     _____

     _____

     _____

     _____

7. Miranda tells Andrea to tell her coworker Emily that she, Andrea, will be going to Paris instead of Emily. She says that if Andrea refuses, she will not work at *Runway* or any other fashion publication. Later, Emily says to Andrea, "You sold your soul the first day you put on those high heels."

   • What does Emily mean?

   _____

   _____

   _____

   _____

   • What does her statement tell us about Andrea's values?

   _____

   _____

   _____

   _____

8. Miranda indicates that she is getting a divorce. She bemoans the bad press and the impact on her twin children. She then goes back to planning dinner arrangements. What does this scene tell us about Miranda?

   _____

   _____

   _____

   _____

9. In this chapter we discuss the notion of the rebirth of an identity.

   • In what way does Andrea have this experience?

   _____

   _____

   _____

   _____

- How do you expect her to be different in the future?

_____

_____

_____

_____

10. How is Miranda the same as and different from the leaders you saw in the other films?

_____

_____

_____

_____

- How do her assumptions—about people, their motivations, and her own behavior—differ from the transformational leaders in the other films?

_____

_____

_____

_____

- What do these assumptions bring out in the people she leads?

_____

_____

_____

_____

11. Take another look at the success scripts described earlier in the "Success Scripts" section of this chapter.
- Which of these scripts do you think describes Miranda best?

_____

_____

_____

_____

- Which success script do the other transformational leaders seem to be following?

_____

_____

_____

_____

- What do you notice about the different outcomes these scripts seem to produce?

_____

_____

_____

_____

12. Describe some insights you gained about personal change and positive organizing from this film and some life experiences that you associate with these insights.

_____

_____

_____

_____

MAKE A JOURNAL ENTRY

Read the following statements. Check the 2 or 3 that resonate most with you.

___1. When our world turns upside down, we are often forced to search out new possibilities and engage in new experiences.

___2. "My sense of identity and my feelings of self-worth were tied directly to the outer circumstances of my life."

___3. Writing or talking about trauma alters how we think about it.

___4. Imagine having confidence that you could enter new situations and bring people together in such a way that a new company emerges.

___5. Turning points capture our attention and invite adaptive self-reflection.

___7. "I am not motivated by rewards; I am purpose-driven."

___8. "I decided I had to be a lot more receptive and a lot more patient."

___9. The leader who has embraced positive reality is able to bring growth where transactional leaders have already given up in frustration.

Now circle the number of the single statement you most resonate with. List some life experiences that you associate with that statement. Then write a paragraph that expresses the importance of one of those life experiences.

Life experiences:

_____

_____

_____

Paragraph:

_____

_____

_____

WRITE A MEMO

Based on your insights, your responses to the questions about the film, and your journal entry, write a short note to someone you know to get across the essence of what you have learned in this chapter.

_____

_____

_____

_____

_____

APPLY THE LEARNING

What are one or two actions you will take to use what you have learned in this chapter about personal change and positive organizing?

_____

_____

_____

_____

_____

CHAPTER FIVE

THE FUNDAMENTAL STATE OF LEADERSHIP

IN THIS CHAPTER

- On the road to deep change, we may experience profound confusion and must learn to cope with uncertainty.
- In our normal state we tend to be comfort-centered, externally directed, self-focused, and internally closed.
- We can shift ourselves into a more influential state by choosing to become more purpose-centered, internally directed, other-focused, and externally open.

When the first edition of *Deep Change* was published, I received many messages from people who were trying to make personal or organizational changes. They wrote that the book helped them move forward in new ways and described how this movement started them on the path to becoming more effective versions of themselves. As more stories arrived, it became clear that a basic pattern recurred in each account of successful, transformative change.

One common theme was that as people reached the midpoint in the deep change process, they felt as if they had strayed from their comfort zone and found themselves trying to make their way through uncertainty. None of them enjoyed feeling disoriented and unsure; nevertheless, they realized that this condition of high challenge was a formative stage in the change process. The tools that had served them in the past no longer sufficed; they had no choice but to search for their core values and decide what they really wanted to achieve.

They were also forced to trust and rely on others. In the same way that a hiker who suspects she is lost must be hyperattentive to environmental clues so she can find her way, people in the midst of deep change must be hypervigilant, carefully considering every bit of feedback they receive. After a time of disorientation, that feedback helps them understand where they are and where they want to go, giving them more confidence in their ability to find their way.

As I read these stories, I started to see the good that could come of feeling lost. In this condition of extreme challenge we are forced to become more virtuous. I mean that in a technical sense: when we face this kind of challenge, we become more committed to a meaningful purpose (courage, engagement, and devotion), more internally directed (integrity, authenticity, and dependability), more other-focused (generosity, compassion, and unity), and more externally open (humility, learning, and optimism). We emerge from the state of extreme challenge with an increased capacity to influence others.

The stories also led me to think about influence from a dynamic perspective. Many people imagine influence as a quality that a person either has or lacks. The stories showed that influence is not a static quality, but something that we gain or lose as we adapt or fail to adapt to the world around us. It seemed that humans are most influential when they are in a condition that I began to call the *fundamental state of leadership*. The fundamental state of leadership is the key to making personal and collective deep change. We can understand it best by contrasting it with our usual way of being, the *normal state*. Most people are in the normal state most of the time. We should not believe ourselves to be exceptions.

A JOURNEY FROM MANAGEMENT TO LEADERSHIP

One student of deep change was Robert Yamamoto, executive director of the Los Angeles Junior Chamber of Commerce. For his first four years in the job, Robert felt good about his accomplishments. Then, a new board president told him that he lacked the leadership capacity necessary to move the organization forward and he would soon be replaced.

The shock Robert experienced served as a turning point. It was the beginning of a personal odyssey of discovery and deep change that began with a great deal of soul searching.

> During the next few months I went through a period of deep introspection. I began to distrust my environment and staff, and I questioned my own management skills and leadership ability. I felt that the board had lost confidence in my ability, so I resigned my position. I became very afraid for myself and my family, and I began to fantasize about ways to somehow keep my job (do it better, faster). I also started to search for a new job.
>
> In the meantime I went to what I thought was my last board meeting. The subject of my resignation came up to the *surprise* of most board members, and interestingly enough, some of the executive committee members. A board member then confronted the president, shared letters of support from stakeholders and my staff, and my role in the organization was reconsidered. [Quinn, 2004, pp. 68–69]

What a happy turn of events! At this point it would have been natural for Robert to feel vindicated and lay the blame for an unpleasant experience on others. Instead, his journey was only beginning. He was about to make a deep commitment and begin seeing his job from an entirely new perspective.

> After that board meeting I did a lot of soul searching. I paid more attention to what I was doing. I began to notice my tendency to gravitate towards routine tasks. I began to see it as a trap. I knew I needed to change. I stopped thinking like a manager and began to think more strategically. I began to commit to achieve larger outcomes. I decided to really lead my organization. It is as if a new person emerged. The decision was not about me. I needed to do it for the good of the organization.
>
> Shortly afterwards, I told the board president, "This is what I must do, this is what the organization must do. If the board doesn't like it, I will leave with no regrets." In the language of *Deep Change,* I was suddenly "walking naked through the land of uncertainty."

To my surprise, she was completely supportive. It was as if a large weight was lifted. I began to see things from multiple perspectives and not just from my own "lens." Learning (not in the traditional sense, but in a holistic sense) became exponential. I saw things with greater clarity and understanding. While before I would need to have a clear understanding of the goal and steps to get there, I trusted my ability to arrive at the destination and learn from the unscripted journey.

There is a universal tendency to call high-level administrators "leaders" simply because they are in positions of authority. Most administrators, however, are like Robert before his transformation. They live in the normal state. They engage in reactive problem solving, emphasize the importance of preserving the hierarchical status quo, minimize personal risk, and avoid leading others into new, unexplored territory. Leaders, by contrast, emphasize creating value, a goal they can only reach if they work to develop new initiatives and try new approaches.

Robert's story describes his personal transition from the management mindset to the leadership perspective. He stopped following the management mentality and began to "build the bridge as he walked on it." The results were profound:

In my new condition I was able to see what had been happening previously. Many people surrounding me were on self-interested journeys. The organization had no unifying goal. The operating strategy was to simply respond to the personal agendas of strong personalities. Roles had been defined through practice and tradition. People often blamed others because they themselves felt insecure and lacked leadership. When I changed, all these things also began to change.

Currently I see myself as a change agent. I have a critical mass of individuals from both the staff and board that are willing to look at our challenges in a new way and work on solutions together. What previously seemed unimaginable now seems to happen with ease. I know it all happened because I confronted my own insecurity, selfishness, and lack of courage.

There is something unusual about the end of Robert's story: he actually knows why his people now engage in positive organizing, why he has a productive community, and why his organization's culture is now productive. Since most of us want to live in such organizations, we should be deeply interested in his answer. Yet his answer is one that few of us are comfortable hearing: "I know it all happened because I confronted my own insecurity, selfishness, and lack of courage."

This statement is profoundly important. Robert did not come up with the painless quick fix that everyone searches for and management books forever promise. Robert chose to change himself. He chose to enter the fundamental state of leadership.

Think About It

- Have you ever had an experience like Robert's? How did you feel? How did you react? What happened?

  _____

  _____

  _____

- If you have never been jolted in this way, try to put yourself in Robert's shoes. How do you think you would feel? How do you think you would react?

  _____

  _____

  _____

- Have you ever worked for an authority figure who behaved more like a manager than a leader? What was the experience like? In what ways did that person's behavior differ from that of a true leader?

  _____

  _____

  _____

THE NORMAL STATE

In moving through life, we all tend to progress and then plateau. At first, the plateau provides time for consolidation and recovery. Later, it becomes a zone of comfort. In our comfort zone we know how to be in control. We handle challenges by relying on what we have learned from experience.

The problem is that the universe is an ever-changing system. From the external world we receive signals suggesting that we need to change, grow beyond our routines, and move to a perspective that embraces a higher level of complexity. Like Robert, we tend to deny these signals. We gravitate toward routine tasks that we know how to do, remaining unaware of the critical changes that are taking place around us. At such times, our influence is not what it might be. Often we need a jolt before we change.

Robert's story is typical. The people around him were on self-interested journeys, the organization had no unifying goal, and the operating strategy was to respond to the personal agendas of strong personalities. Roles were defined by tradition. Blame was rampant because people felt insecure and projected their insecurities onto others.

This describes the normal organizational condition, whether the organization is a Fortune 500 company or the local school district. In fact, self-interested exchange and the lack of excellence are so common that we expect and accept them. We usually prefer not to see that everyone is colluding to avoid the pursuit of excellence. (See Figure 5.1.)

Failing to change is often part of a process in which we react to changing signals from the world around us by cutting ourselves off from further information. As we become increasingly closed, we lose energy and hope. We become afraid and insecure, we are filled with doubts about our capacity to learn our way forward, and we resort to denial that shuts out more of the signals from evolving external realities, becoming increasingly cut off and losing still more energy. We become trapped in a vicious cycle. We deny that we are losing vitality. We work to stay in our comfort zone. But staying in our comfort zone means we can only imitate that which has been done in the past. We see ourselves as a noun rather than a verb. We are less able to adapt to emerging realities.

In our organizations the same dynamics come into play. We spend most of our time unconsciously colluding in the diminishment of the organization. We lose hope, tend to self-interest, and experience increased conflict. Cut off from the reality emerging around it, the organization loses energy at an accelerating rate.

At both the individual and the organizational levels we tend to choose slow death over deep change. Slow death is the consequence of remaining in the

FIGURE 5.1   The Normal State

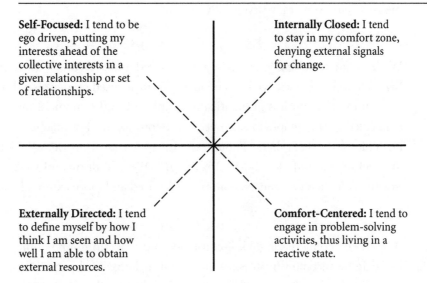

Self-Focused: I tend to be ego driven, putting my interests ahead of the collective interests in a given relationship or set of relationships.

Internally Closed: I tend to stay in my comfort zone, denying external signals for change.

Externally Directed: I tend to define myself by how I think I am seen and how well I am able to obtain external resources.

Comfort-Centered: I tend to engage in problem-solving activities, thus living in a reactive state.

normal state. To be in the normal state is to be comfort-centered, externally directed, self-focused, and internally closed.

It's Normal to Be Comfort-Centered

We seek to keep doing what we know how to do. If we are not successful, we may have to learn new assumptions and routines. But we are often more committed to the comfort of what we know than to attaining excellence, which requires us to change. At GM, the executives were trapped in their old assumptions. In the film *Moneyball* (Chapter Two), the scouts believed that they wanted to build a winning baseball team. But they were not willing to consider new ideas to do so. Instead, they became resistant. We all tend to be like those executives and those scouts.

It's Normal to Be Externally Directed

We know from experience that we must survive in a system of social exchange. We saw this illustrated in the film *Norma Rae* (Chapter One), where Norma's identity formed around the expectations others held for her. Because we are very influenced by what we think certain others are thinking about us, we go to great lengths to respond to what we think they are thinking. As we become more familiar with what they think about us—a straightforward task in a stable environment—we become more externally driven.

It's Normal to Be Focused on Our Own Needs

We have a natural tendency to be self-centered and self-conscious. In moments of high self-consciousness, we become increasingly focused on our own thoughts, worries, and goals, and less authentically connected to the moment and less directly connected to the people in our network. Soon, we are less able to solve problems and enlist the aid of others. Though we want external approval, we fail to obtain it. We feel increasingly lonely. We feel angry. We withdraw and we feel still more isolated. We then become even more self-focused and more externally driven.

It's Normal to Be Internally Closed

As we become increasingly self-conscious and strive to impress others, we call on our defense mechanisms to shut out signals calling for change. We saw this illustrated in the life of Andrea (*The Devil Wears Prada*, Chapter Four) when she kept telling people, "I had no choice."

Andrea's behavior occurs in everyone. Yet when we deploy such defense mechanisms we tend to become more insecure and more closed. The moment at which we most need to be externally open is often the moment when we are the most closed.

Think About It

• Drawing on the descriptions of a normal state in this section, how would you describe your current state? Be as honest and objective as you can.

_____

_____

_____

• If your description indicates that you are currently in a normal state, what might happen if you were to enter a state of deep change?

_____

_____

_____

THE FUNDAMENTAL STATE OF LEADERSHIP

You already know that remaining in the normal state, refusing to change while the universe changes around us, is ultimately choosing slow death. To enter the fundamental state of leadership is to become more purpose-centered, internally directed, other-focused, and externally open.

We Become Less Comfort-Centered, More Purpose-Centered

We achieve this by asking the important question, "What result do I want to create?" (Fritz, 1989, p. 68). An honest answer tends to create an image or vision that may attract us outside our comfort zone onto the uncertain journey that results in commitment, learning, growth, and development. As we begin to pursue purpose in the face of uncertainty, we gain a sense of meaning, hope, and energy. We experience meaning and become filled with positive emotions. (See Figure 5.2.)

FIGURE 5.2   The Fundamental State of Leadership

Other-Focused: I am transcending my ego, putting the common good and welfare of others first, increasing in authenticity and transparency, nurturing trust, and enriching the levels of connectivity in my networks.

Externally Open: I am moving outside my comfort zone, experimenting, seeking real feedback, adapting, and reaching exponentially higher levels of discovery, awareness, competence, and vision.

Internally Directed: I am continually examining my hypocrisy and closing the gaps between my values and behavior. I am reaching higher levels of personal security and confidence.

Purpose-Centered: I am clarifying what result I want to create. I am committed and engaged, full of energy and holding an unwavering standard as I pursue a meaningful task.

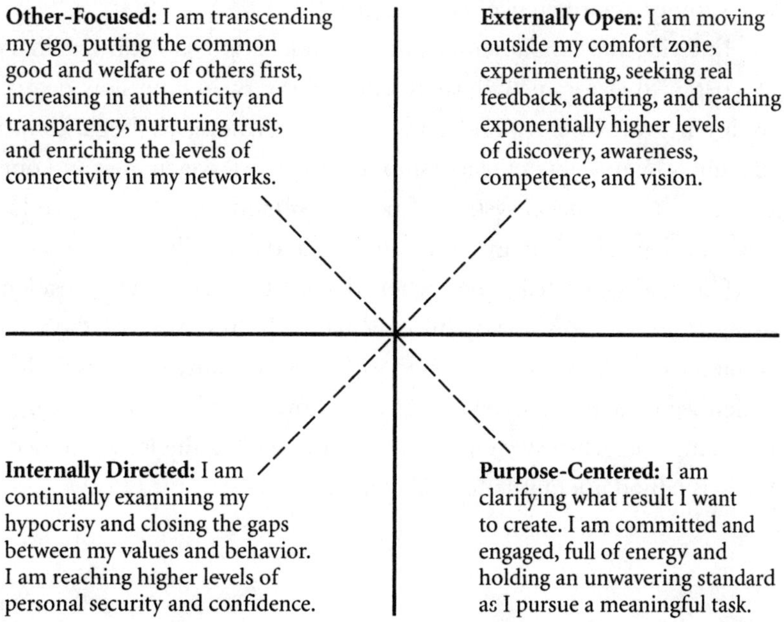

We Become Less Externally Directed, More Internally Directed

We begin to confront our own hypocrisy, closing the gap between who we think we are and who we think we should be. This victory over self gives us greater integrity and causes us to feel more whole. Values and behavior become more congruent. Our internal and external realities become more aligned, and we reach higher levels of security and confidence.

We Become Less Self-Focused, More Other-Focused

With an increasing sense of concern and unity that helps us feel more secure, we can put the common good and welfare of others ahead of the preservation of self. The collective interest becomes our new self-interest. Our relationships tend to increase in meaning, trust, and caring.

We Become Less Internally Closed, More Externally Open

When we meet our needs for increased achievement, integrity, and affiliation, we increase our confidence that we can learn our way forward in an uncertain world. Such adaptive confidence makes us genuinely open to all forms of feedback. We are better able to embrace the truth of the dynamic world. We then further grow in awareness, competence, and vision.

Entering the fundamental state of leadership is an extraordinary thing to do. We begin to attract new flows of energy. We overcome slow death. We feel that we are moving forward and growing. Furthermore, we begin to attract others to the fundamental state of leadership. Like Robert, we change and our organization changes. It becomes a system of positive organizing, a more productive community with increased energy, commitment, and capability.

Consider what happened when Robert told the board president that he was going to execute his new plans or leave with "no regrets": the woman who had wanted to fire him now expressed support. By changing himself, he changed her. When we change ourselves, we change how people see and respond to us. When we change ourselves, we change the world. This is the legacy of people who operate in the fundamental state of leadership.

Think About It

- Consider each of the four characteristics of the fundamental state of leadership. How would your life be different today if you increased in each of these characteristics? Select a key character from one of the films (Reuben, Norma, Billy Beane, Lionel, or Andrea) or a key character in your life and indicate a time when the person became more of the following:

Purpose-centered:

_____

_____

_____

_____

Internally directed:

_____

_____

_____

_____

Other-focused:

_____

_____

_____

_____

Externally open:

_____

_____

_____

_____

BECOMING ALIGNED WITH THE DYNAMIC UNIVERSE

When we clarify what result we want to create, live from our values, maintain high-quality relationships, and become externally open, we can move forward successfully with limited knowledge or control. We enter a state of elevated attention and learning. One important reason for the successes of people in the fundamental state of leadership is that they begin to care more deeply about what they are trying to accomplish than about the preservation of their ego. When we enter the fundamental state of leadership we look for any information that will allow us to move forward more effectively. As a result, we may come to dramatic new insights about ourselves and the organization. When we release our fears and embrace the learning process, titles and roles tend to melt away. In relationships of trust and learning we are able to recognize new resources.

In his story, Robert says, "While before I would need to have a clear understanding of the goal and steps to get there, I trusted my ability to arrive at the destination, and learn from the unscripted journey." When we embark on this unscripted journey, we become a creative and adaptive system that is in dynamic connection with a constantly changing universe. We attract energy and expand in awareness. We know what result we want to create and we move toward it, even if we do not know how to get there. In this state of increased integrity, courage, and energy, we are leading in the most powerful way possible.

Personal Reflection and Application

REFLECT

While the chapter is fresh in your mind, quickly write down the 4 to 6 points, concepts, or ideas that stand out for you the most.

WATCH THE FILM: *REMEMBER THE TITANS*

Life is full of conflict. Friendships, marriages, organizations, and entire societies decay because conflict is not transformed into cooperation. This is a key task for every leader. In this movie we watch a leader transform conflict into cooperation. Boys who have been socialized to hate each other learn to find purpose, clarify values, increase connection, and move forward into uncertainty, learning as they go. In short, they are enticed into the fundamental state of leadership by a coach who is in the fundamental state of leadership. The process turns the conflicted boys into champions.

Questions to Consider

1. Early in the movie Coach Boone arrives in the office of Coach Yoast and his assistant. A number of aggressive comments are made. Someone in the normal state might have been offended and reacted negatively, and the conversation may have turned into a conflict. How does Coach Boone shape the conversation and keep it productive?

_____

_____

_____

_____

2. Before leaving for camp, Gerry, the captain of the white team, approaches Coach Boone. He demands that half the offense and the entire defense be white players.

   • How would a person in the normal state react?

_____

_____

_____

_____

- How did Coach Boone respond?

_____

_____

_____

_____

- What was the outcome?

_____

_____

_____

_____

3. At Gettysburg Coach Boone gives a speech about the destructive nature of hatred and the potential in the boys. What is different about this kind of communication? What does it take for a person to make this kind of statement?

_____

_____

_____

_____

4. As they left for camp the football team was highly conflicted. By the time they got back, they were singing together.

- List the things that account for this transformation.

_____

_____

_____

_____

- Given your list, what are the principles for guiding transformational change?

_____

_____

_____

_____

5. On the first day of school it becomes apparent that many powerful forces are working to destroy what was accomplished at camp.

   • What were those forces?

   _____

   _____

   _____

   • How are the dynamics at work in this story relevant to other organizations?

   _____

   _____

   _____

6. Coach Boone claims that Coach Yoast is patronizing the young black players and therefore crippling them for life. What was right about the positions of both coaches?

   _____

   _____

   _____

   _____

7. As the season unfolds, the team meets without any coaches. How and why is this significant to the development of the team?

   _____

   _____

   _____

   _____

8. As the team succeeds, surprising changes occur. The police officer, for example, stops Julius and compliments the defense; the neighbors cheer Coach Boone.

- What do such changes signify?

  _____

  _____

  _____

- What similarities might we see in the transformation of a business or agency?

  _____

  _____

  _____

9. Identify times when Coach Boone was:
   - Purpose-centered:

     _____

     _____

     _____

   - Internally directed:

     _____

     _____

     _____

   - Other-focused:

     _____

     _____

     _____

   - Externally open:

     _____

     _____

     _____

10. Describe some insights you derive about the fundamental state of leadership from this film and some life experiences that you associate with these insights.

_____

_____

_____

MAKE A JOURNAL ENTRY

Read the following statements. Check the 2 or 3 that resonate most with you.

___1. As people reach the midpoint in the deep change process, they feel as if they have strayed from their comfort zone.

___2. People in the midst of deep change must be hypervigilant to every bit of feedback they receive.

___3. Influence is not a static quality but something that we gain or lose as we adapt or fail to adapt to the world around us.

___4. "I know it all happened because I confronted my own insecurity, selfishness, and lack of courage."

___5. Self-interested exchange and lack of excellence are so common that we expect and accept them.

___6. Staying in our comfort zone means we can only imitate that which has been done in the past.

___7. Remaining in the normal state—refusing to change while the universe changes around us—is ultimately to choose slow death.

___8. In the normal state, we deny the emergence of the slow death phenomenon while we ourselves exemplify it.

___9. Instead of asking, "What do I want?" we must ask, "What result do I want to create?"

___10. Others are transformed because our increased virtues become a catalyst of collective change.

Now circle the number of the single statement you most resonate with. List some life experiences that you associate with that statement. Then write a paragraph that expresses the importance of one of those life experiences.

Life experiences:

_____

_____

_____

Paragraph:

_____

_____

_____

WRITE A MEMO

Based on your insights, your responses to the questions about the film, and your journal entry, write a short note to someone you know. Help them understand the essence of what you have learned in this chapter.

_____

_____

_____

APPLY THE LEARNING

What are one or two actions you will take to use what you have learned in this chapter and move closer to the fundamental state of leadership?

_____

_____

_____

CHAPTER SIX

MORAL POWER

- Every organization has a technical system, a political system, and a moral system. The first two are readily recognized, the third is not.
- When leadership fails, the moral system collapses and the people become self-interested.
- People of increased authenticity are people who have embraced their own power and have the capacity to invite others to embrace their own power.
- When conversations become authentic, the moral system repairs itself and the organization finds the power to change.

Slow death is a normal organizational process. Unless work is done to the contrary, organizations move toward rigidity or chaos. To avoid slow death, an organization must move into a state of adaptive order. This order emerges when the people in an organization pursue a vision. It is a vision of how to tend to the evolving needs of the people outside the organization—the clients or customers. It is a vision that orients people inside the organization to the common good of the organization and inspires them to sacrifice for it. When this double-edged vision is embraced, the order becomes adaptive.

In such an organization people are centered in the present and also oriented to the emergent future. They learn and change in real time. To maintain this adaptive order the people must transcend the self-interested conflicts that occur in hierarchies. As was illustrated in *Remember the Titans*, this is done not by avoiding conflicts but by surfacing conflicts and transcending them.

This kind of order overcomes entropy because work has been done to the contrary. That work is moral in nature. It is based not on the politics of a given situation but on enactment of ethical principles. Leaders bring about adaptive order by becoming adaptive people. Adaptive people become leaders when they enter the fundamental state of leadership. An individual can choose to become purpose-centered, internally directed, other-focused, and externally open. Adaptive order results from a process of self-change.

In a world of normal assumptions, it is difficult to grasp the notion of self-change and adaptive order. So in this chapter we consider the case of a woman trying to operate under extreme circumstances. As she does, she finds the courage to change herself. As she becomes a more internally directed person, everything changes.

AN EXTREME SITUATION

Gail is a practicing psychologist who works with me as one of several facilitators in an executive education course that is designed to be an experience in authentic communication. The first two hours of the course prepare people to tell three stories that communicate the essence of who they are. Before they tell their stories to one another, the facilitators model authenticity by telling stories of their own. The stories are usually about difficult experiences, personal failures, or life-changing choices—things that most people are hesitant to share but benefit from discussing openly.

Gail's story is about what happened the first time she acted as one of the facilitators in this course. Here is her account as recorded in my book, *Building the Bridge As You Walk On It* (Quinn, 2004, pp. 29–33):

> On the first day, Bob asked us to break up into small groups and tell stories of an important event that had shaped us in some way. My job was to share my story first to demonstrate the process. I had purposefully not planned a story in advance and shared one that was personal in nature, but felt safe for me to tell.

We were instructed to do three rounds of storytelling and observe what occurred in each round. Not surprisingly, with each round of story-telling we became more intimate in our revelations. With that intimacy came feelings of vulnerability. Our defenses were coming down.

That afternoon, Bob shared a story about a successful woman who, after leaving an abusive marriage, learned to be very discerning in her choice of whom to date, eventually enjoying a successful relationship. The class then discussed this question: "If you transform yourself, can you change an abusive relationship, either personally or organizationally, into a loving and/or respectful one?"

In keeping with my commitment to be open and authentic, I sponta-neously intervened with a story about my decision to leave an abusive husband.

My first husband was a verbally, emotionally, and physically abusive man. I had grown to fear him and was as careful as I knew how to be [in order] not to trigger his rages.

One evening, when I arrived home after being late to pick him up after work, he was waiting for me with a leather belt in his hand. He be-gan screaming obscenities and beating me with the belt. As usual I was totally unprepared and unable or unwilling to defend myself. As usual, I felt victimized.

I am not certain how long the attack continued, but at some point, something inside me literally clicked. Time slowed down, and I remember hearing a voice inside me say as clearly as if there had been someone in the room talking to me, "You know he's crazy, but you must be crazy too for putting up with this." In that moment, I was transformed from the victim of an abusive husband to a woman who had choices, and I knew, even though I was not ready emotionally or financially, that I would leave the relationship.

I never said a word or lifted a finger to defend myself, but the most amazing thing happened. He stopped hitting me and screaming at me, dropped the belt, and walked away. We never spoke of the incident, and he never again raised his voice to me or lifted a finger to harm me. It was as if he somehow sensed that he would never be able to treat me that way again.

In a moment of profound awareness, I had taken personal responsibility for my own sense of well-being, and I had changed on a deep, fundamental level. Within months I had enrolled in graduate school, moved out of our apartment, and filed for divorce. I had changed the world by changing myself.

Think About It

- What do you think happened in Gail's moment of transformation to cause her husband to stop beating her and treating her in a negative way?

_____

_____

_____

- What does it mean to become more internally directed?

_____

_____

_____

- Do you see ways in which Gail's story is relevant to you as a leader in an organization? In what ways is it relevant?

_____

_____

_____

THE IMPACT OF ENTERING THE FUNDAMENTAL STATE OF LEADERSHIP

I find Gail's story of her moment of decision to be breathtaking. At first glance, you might think the story has little to do with leadership or organizations. But Gail's story has relevance in professional life. People in organizations, from the bottom to the top, often feel disempowered. They report being trapped into behaving in self-defeating ways because they are intimidated by some authority figure, some difficult political situation, or some other constraint. They tend to develop well-polished rationalizations to explain why they cannot do the right thing. Like Gail, they feel immobilized.

Gail believed that she was in a situation over which she had no control. With no choices, she could only submit. Then, in a profound moment, she realized that choices were open to her. She could choose to make a change. At that moment, she entered the fundamental state of leadership. She became internally directed and took responsibility for herself. She changed at a fundamental level.

Now consider the amazing impact: at the moment she decided to change, her husband stopped screaming, dropped the belt, and walked away. How can we explain this extraordinary effect?

We communicate more than the words we say. We continually broadcast implicit messages. When we enter the fundamental state of leadership, we broadcast new messages. When we become more focused, people respond to our purposiveness. When we become internally directed, as did Gail, we communicate that we have embraced our deepest values and we are no longer afraid. When we are more other-focused, we send a message of empathetic understanding, and people respond to our concern. When we are more externally open, we send a message of humility, and people recognize our genuine desire for feedback and learning.

Thoreau describes something similar in his essay "Civil Disobedience":

Action from principle, the perception and the performance of right, changes things and relations; it is essentially revolutionary, and does not consist wholly with anything that was. It not only divides states and churches, it divides families; aye, it divides the individual, separating the diabolical in him from the divine. [1993, p. 7]

Why is it that "action from principle, the perception and the performance of right" represents radical change? Choosing to be internally directed, to live from principle, is the beginning of change. It is choosing to create, rather than accept, the future. Doing this separates, divides, and changes relationships. When we claim our integrity and exercise the courage to enter the fundamental state of leadership, we leave behind existing patterns of social exchange. We become creative actors working to bring about something radically new.

Gail moved to this fundamental place. She chose to claim her unique self, the self of highest potential. She chose to engage in the "performance of right." This is always revolutionary act. Why? For the same reason Thoreau gave: "It does not consist wholly with anything that was."

When we, like Gail, choose to move toward a new and a better future, we become more virtuous. We see more virtue in others, and we attract people toward greater virtue. We become catalysts of change. As we create a better and more complex self, we destroy some existing social arrangements. Those around us must change their behavior as the expectations that previously guided them in their interactions with us cease to apply.

Think About It
- Even small acts can be revolutionary in making a radical break with the past. Can you think of an example from your own experience that illustrates the statement, "Action from principle, the perception and performance of right . . . does not consist wholly with anything that was"?

_____

_____

_____

A SECOND TRANSFORMATION

It turns out that sharing her story sparked another transformation for Gail.

> Prior to my participation as a facilitator in the class, I had never shared that story with anyone—not my parents, my current husband, or any of my closest friends. I had buried the memory of that incident, and along with it the feelings of humiliation and shame I felt.
>
> Before I could feel regret or embarrassment about what I had shared in a very public forum, Bob said the most amazing thing. He said, "That is an incredibly powerful story. Thank you for sharing it."

To quote Bob, I had "walked naked into the land of uncertainty," sharing a story that I had always regarded as a sign of weakness. In the telling I watched the story transform into a story of courage and strength. In the telling, which was itself an act of courage, my perspective shifted, and I saw for the first time my courage and strength in that situation.

It has been almost one year since I participated in that class, and I would say the fundamental change in me is my willingness to lovingly and wholeheartedly embrace those parts of me that I have regarded as flawed. Sharing and being affirmed for sharing has transformed those flaws and weaknesses into strengths. Clearly my clients have benefited from this shift because I am much better able to help them embrace their weaknesses and flaws and transform them into strengths. My family and friends also benefit because I am much less guarded and defensive, more willing to be open and vulnerable, and have a greater sense of self-esteem, all of which allows for greater intimacy and closeness.

Because she was ashamed of her story, Gail had never shared it. When she did she made a startling discovery. She discovered that her story of change was a story of courage, power, and strength. She says that telling the story released her from a long-held belief that she was not good enough. The change, she adds, "has opened many doors that were formerly locked away, freeing me to become a more fully effective version of myself and therefore more effective in all that I do."

In the fundamental state of leadership we become purpose-centered, internally directed, other-focused, and externally open. If we choose to move on one dimension we tend to move on the others as well. Gail has become a person of purpose. She is internally directed, now courageously living from her values. She is other-focused, intimate, and connected with her family. She is externally open, reporting being "less guarded and defensive, more willing to be open and vulnerable." In such a state she signals that she is ready to continually learn and adapt.

Think About It

Gail engaged in self-change. In an extreme situation, she chose to act courageously on her core values. This caused her husband to stop abusing her. It also changed the nature of her professional and family life.

- Have you ever been in a difficult situation and then made the choice to become more internally directed? What happened?

  _____

  _____

  _____

- In what part of your life do you currently need to be more internally directed?

  _____

  _____

  _____

BECOMING WHAT YOU BEHOLD AND BEHOLDING WHAT YOU BECOME

The great visionary poet and artist William Blake, whose career spanned the turn of the nineteenth century, was deeply concerned with the idea of transformation. Blake was a revolutionary in the sense that he believed society needed not just superficial reform but profound change. He did not believe that political action alone would bring about radical change. Political revolutions, he noted, have a way of reestablishing the tyranny they were intended to overthrow. Instead, the idea of revolution had to come first of all in people's thinking and being. Truly meaningful change would happen only when people awoke to the infinite potential that was inside them.

In Blake's mythical language, the world that I have described as the normal state is described as "fallen." It is the world of self-concern, routine, conformity, and hypocrisy. Our longing for a more virtuous world is a sign that a better world is possible.

Most of us, however, see the normal world as something to accept and conform to, much as Gail once accepted her husband's abuse. When we are in that state of passive acceptance, our view of ourselves diminishes. According to Blake, that is because our relationship with the world around us is reciprocal: the reality we perceive and the view we have of ourselves feed on one another. Describing this relationship, he wrote: "They became what they beheld." When we accept the world as it is (that is, when we are in the normal state), we deny our innate ability to see something better, and hence our ability to *be* something better. The better world we seek can be found within us, if only we change our vision (Kazin, 1974, p. 487):

> In your own Bosom you bear your Heaven
> And Earth & all you behold; tho' it appears Without, it is Within

Gail's story is an example of this. When she made the decisive commitment to transform herself from a victim into an active, powerful agent, the world changed with her. If there was no victim, then there was no abuser with the power to harm. In a sense, what she beheld came to be.

Personal Reflection and Application

WATCH THE FILM: *STAND AND DELIVER*

This is the story of an organization that is performing far below its potential. The organization's culture is dysfunctional. Administrators claim they want change but behave in ways that prevent change. Both the organization and its employees are stuck in the slow death process. Then Mr. Escalante, a new teacher, enters the system. He is different from the other teachers. He lives in the fundamental state of leadership. Because of him, the organization begins to change. The film challenges the common assumption that organizations must be changed from the top and illustrates the dynamics that emerge when someone provides real leadership.

Questions to Consider

1. Think about what was going on in the organization before Mr. Escalante arrived.

   - What were the conditions in the school and the classroom? What did you see that indicates that the organization was experiencing slow death?

_____

_____

_____

_____

- What normal kinds of changes were the authority figures trying to make? Why were they having limited success?

_____

_____

_____

_____

- How were they like the executives at GM we read about in Chapter One?

_____

_____

_____

_____

2. While others failed to create change, Mr. Escalante was able to bring about a dramatic transformation in the organization.

- Was he results-focused? What was his vision?

_____

_____

_____

_____

- Was he internally directed? What role did his values play?

_____

_____

_____

_____

- Was he other focused? How much did he care?

_____

_____

_____

- Was he externally open? How did his strategy evolve?

_____

_____

_____

- What in his background and present life made it possible for him to behave differently from others?

_____

_____

_____

3. How did Mr. Escalante exercise moral power? What kinds of resistance emerged? How does the statement from Thoreau apply to this case?

_____

_____

_____

4. Mr. Escalante's behavior offers a model of how to create deep change. What does he have in common with the other transformational leaders observed in the previous films?

_____

_____

_____

5. Think of at least three things Mr. Escalante did to capture attention, demonstrate credibility, and build commitment? What principles do you derive from his example?

_____

_____

_____

6. What new resources emerged as he moved forward?

_____

_____

_____

7. What were the long-term outcomes of his efforts on individual people, the school, and the community?

_____

_____

_____

8. List the key insights about moral power you gained from the film and briefly describe life experiences that you associate with these insights.

_____

_____

_____

MAKE A JOURNAL ENTRY

Read the following statements. Check the 2 or 3 that resonate most with you.

___1. "In a moment of profound awareness, I had taken personal responsibility for my own sense of well-being, and I had changed on a deep, fundamental level."

___2. Executives sometimes take on a victim mentality to avoid having to make deep change.

___3. "Action from principle, the perception and the performance of right, changes things and relations."

___4. "In the telling, which was itself an act of courage, my perspective shifted, and I saw for the first time my courage and strength in that situation."

___5. Our most unique characteristics have the greatest potential for bonding us.

___6. Truly meaningful change will happen only when people awaken to the infinite potential that is inside them.

___7. When we accept the world as it is (that is, when we are in the normal state), we deny our innate ability to see something better, and hence our ability to be something better.

___8. The better world we seek can be found within us, if only we change our vision.

Now circle the number of the single statement you most resonate with. List some life experiences that you associate with that statement. Then write a paragraph that expresses the importance of one of those life experiences.

Life experiences:

_____

_____

_____

Paragraph:

_____

_____

_____

WRITE A MEMO

Based on your insights, your responses to the questions about the film, and your journal entry, write a short note to someone you know to convey the essence of what you have learned in this chapter.

_____

_____

_____

_____

_____

APPLY THE LEARNING

What are one or two actions you will take from what you have learned in this chapter as the next steps on your journey of mastering the deep change process?

_____

_____

_____

_____

_____

CHAPTER SEVEN

LEADERSHIP AND POSITIVITY

IN THIS CHAPTER

- Every organization, group, and relationship is subject to the problem of self-interest.
- Organizations prosper when leaders inspire people to transcend their own self-interest and sacrifice for the common good.
- At the heart of the developmental process is positive emotion in the leader and positive emotion in the people.
- A leader's task is to help people find the image that will draw them into the positive creation of their own future.

In early 2011, when Greece was in an economic crisis, I was invited to speak to three hundred Greek business leaders on the topic, "Positive Leadership in Troubled Times." I gave the talk.

The next day, I had a private tour of the Agora, the old marketplace just below the Acropolis. I found it very inspiring to stand in the place where the notion of democracy had been born and where many of the fundamental concepts of Western life developed. I was also inspired by my guide's tales of Socrates, who had so much integrity that he was willing to die for his beliefs. Though his accusers thought otherwise, he was invested in the common good of his country.

Some of the social mechanisms that were created in those times still influence governance today. Others, such as the formal process of ostracism, have been discarded. Ostracism is an interesting example of an institution that, over time, began to be used in problematic ways. Originally intended to protect democracy by temporarily exiling people who were consolidating too much power and influence, the practice was soon corrupted by those in power who wanted to eliminate others whose growing influence might pose a challenge to their rule. A practice that was invented to improve democracy became a means by which rulers could put their own good over the good of the collective.

At the time of my visit, Greece faced immense external pressure to change, yet the people seemed unable to change. Politicians and bureaucrats had been on the take for centuries, and the citizens had learned how to avoid paying taxes. Corruption had infected both the collective culture and the individual citizens. This cycle of self-interest was the same slow death process that we have been examining throughout this field guide. Even though the country was nearing bankruptcy, no one was willing to sacrifice for the common good. Lacking hope that others would change and not trusting them to do their part, everyone pursued their own personal good. This further undermined trust, creating a vicious cycle that prevented unity.

With this observation came an insight. Every organization, group, and relationship is subject to the tyranny of self-interest. Organizations prosper when leaders inspire people to transcend their own self-interests and sacrifice for the common good. After thousands of years, we should have mastered this most central skill. We have not. After many decades of scientific work on leadership, our professional schools should instill this skill in every student. They do not. Most professional schools claim to teach leadership but totally ignore the engine of leadership: the internalized commitment to moral power that makes influence transformational. The dominance of the assumptions of normal organizing in professional education and practice hinders the development of transformational leadership.

Think About It

- Why does destructive self-interest arise so often in organizations?

_____

_____

_____

- How can self-interest be transformed into pursuit of the collective interest?

  _____

  _____

  _____

- What does personal integrity have to do with transformational leadership?

  _____

  _____

  _____

A TERRIBLE REALIZATION

When I returned home I wrote two blog entries (www.leadingwithlift.com/blog). The first contained the essence of what is written in the opening paragraphs of this chapter. In the second, I sought to answer the question, "Do I ever contribute to the corruption of the collective?"

I explained that I had gone to Greece to speak to discouraged business leaders on how to find opportunity in troubled conditions. Although the talk was reasonably well-received, I considered it a failure. I was speaking about the fundamental state of leadership, but I was not in that fundamental state. I was in the normal state. I was comfort-centered, externally directed, self-focused, and internally closed. Thus, I was unable to help those three hundred people initiate the transformation of the Greek economy. But how could I have done that impossible task?

The answer can be found in the history of great transformations. Change requires a vibrant organizing image. A particularly good illustration comes from Nelson Mandela in his book, _Long Walk to Freedom_ (1994).

In the 1950s there was little hope for the freedom-seeking efforts of black South Africans. Then, in 1955, an innovative idea was introduced: a "Congress of the People" representing every group in the country would draw up a charter containing principles for the creation of a new South Africa. It was a new organizing image.

People from two hundred organizations were asked, "If you could make the laws . . . what would you do?" Asking the people to envision their own future caught the collective imagination and gave rise to a national conversation about purpose, integrity, connection, and learning. Suggestions came from everywhere. The document that emerged was short, clear, and inspiring. It became an organizing image that would endure through a very long period of agony and eventually would lead to the emergence of the new South Africa.

The African National Congress's leadership of South Africa's transformation showed me what I should have done in Greece. I should have asked the business leaders to discuss the question, "What do you want Greece to be?" At the time, I believe such a discussion would have been briefly resisted and then it would have exploded with energy. I could have then invited the participants to go home and invite people in their companies and all other organizations to share their answers to this question. That viral process might have resulted in a new organizing image that would most likely have called for change in all aspects of Greek life. As in South Africa, much tribulation would follow, but the spreading conversation might result in the gradual emergence of purpose (commitment), integrity, connection, and openness to learning in real time.

The skeptic will respond that I present a simplistic and unrealistic concept. A financial expert who actually lived through the agonies of the Greek process would likely agree.

My reply is that the approach is simple but not unrealistic. Skeptics are seldom people of vision. They spend very little time in the fundamental state of leadership. If they did, they would better understand that leadership binds realism to optimism and concern for results with concern for relationships, while stimulating the complex process of development. The crisis in Greece was an organic change process, and the people needed an organizing image just as the people in South Africa did and used it to pull themselves through their agonies and into their desired future.

The lesson of my trip to Greece was that self-interest has been corrupting organizations for as long as they have existed. Real leadership is pursuing the common good of the system. People who are in the fundamental state of leadership invite others to transcend their normal assumptions of self-interest, external rewards, exchange, conflict, alienation, and scarcity. They act on new assumptions of sacrifice for the common good, intrinsic rewards, exceeding expectations, possibility, trust, and expanded resources.

Think About It

- What made the Freedom Charter so powerful?

  _____

  _____

  _____

- What is the role of conversation in the process of change?

  _____

  _____

  _____

- Why did I fail to start a transformational dialogue with the Greek business leaders?

  _____

  _____

  _____

- Identify a time when you failed as I failed.

  _____

  _____

  _____

THE ROLE OF POSITIVE EMOTIONS IN LEADING CHANGE

I was once invited to run a business school retreat at a university. The faculty wanted to set a positive tone by creating shared aspirations. One of my colleagues had given the same group a presentation a year earlier, including a series of empirical findings on positive organizing as well as tools that could be used to apply the principles he was teaching. People had been very impressed. One professor told me that the presentation had left him feeling "intellectually awed."

But few of my colleagues' suggestions had actually been applied, and the general attitude was gloomy. It had been a tough year for the school's finances. It had also been a year of conflict between some faculty members and the dean's office. This kind of conflict tends to perpetuate itself, and makes it difficult for people to move from living under normal assumptions to enacting the assumptions of positive organizing.

When I felt the tension in the room, I began to worry that I would not succeed. Each time a possible strategy came to mind, a troublesome inner voice would indicate why it would fail. In this negative state, I could see no options.

I knew I had to transform my own negative feelings into positive emotions. If I was going to initiate change, I had to change. I thought of the work of Barbara Fredrickson (2009). Her research efforts demonstrate that positive emotions are necessary to openness and learning. Some of these emotions are joy, gratitude, serenity, interest, hope, pride, amusement, inspiration, awe, and love.

Frederickson's research indicates that these emotions lead to thoughts that are unusual and flexible, integrate differences, and are more efficient. When we increase the flow of positive emotions, we can envision more possibilities. Positive emotions improve our ability to cope with adversity and make us more likely to find positive meaning in what is going on around us, even when we are surrounded by negative processes. They facilitate planning and goal-setting; they also increase our ability to play, explore, savor experiences, and integrate new views into the self. Thus, positivity helps us make deep personal change and transform ourselves and our organizations. People become more integrated, more capable, and more resilient when things go wrong.

We can access these desirable outcomes by increasing something Frederickson calls the *positivity ratio*, which is the frequency of positive feelings over a given period divided by the frequency of negative feelings over the same period.

Fredrickson found that there is a tipping point around which the effects of the positivity ratio change dramatically. When we experience fewer than three positive feelings for each negative feeling, we tend to spiral downward and become increasingly rigid. We feel overwhelmed as we lose energy, and we slip into the pattern of slow death. Above the ratio of three to one, we are pulled into upward spirals. We become increasingly open and creative. By monitoring and regulating our positivity ratio, we can determine whether we are slowly moving toward stagnation and death or toward learning, growth, and development. It is a choice that determines our quality of life.

Think About It

- Consider times when you have been especially creative. Where were you? What were you doing? What feelings were you experiencing before and during this period of creativity?

  _____

  _____

  _____

- Does your behavior change when your mind is filled with positive thoughts? In what ways?

  _____

  _____

  _____

- Have you ever tried to increase the number of positive thoughts you have? What activities, mental or physical, helped you have those thoughts?

  _____

  _____

  _____

ALTERING THE POSITIVITY RATIO

I often work on my own positivity ratio. When I have a negative feeling or thought, I consciously choose to replace it with a positive thought. I sometimes try to hold my mind in a positive place by repeating a long quotation that inspires me. Most of the time I use the following four questions:

- What result do I want to create?
- Am I internally directed?

- Am I other-focused?
- Am I externally open?

While waiting to present at the business school retreat, I used all these techniques to prepare myself. As I sat in the audience, I also listened to the early presentations. One was given by a woman named Kathy, who described herself as "just a staff person." Kathy was responsible for a small department in the business school. Such people are often treated as if they are invisible.

At first, Kathy was tentative. She had been particularly impressed by the research that my colleague had presented on the topic of gratitude the year before. He had taught the group that one of the most powerful interventions we can make in our lives is to keep a gratitude journal. Kathy described how this advice made such a difference in her personal life that she brought the concept to work. She established "Thankful Thursdays," on which day everyone in her group shared highlights from their gratitude journals. Some people had been cynical and resistant at first, saying things like "This is corny." But she persisted.

As Kathy described the changes that had taken place in her unit, her demeanor changed. She appeared confident and full of joy. Then something even more impressive happened. The audience members from her department began spontaneously to express themselves, sharing stories of how the department had changed.

I was impressed by Kathy's story. Yet even though I had been continually exposed to research that documents the value of a gratitude journal, I had never bothered to start one for myself; I, like so many others, tend to avoid self-change.

Then I had an experience that got my attention. During a meeting with some professional colleagues, a highly accomplished woman named Schon told us that she had kept a gratitude journal for eighteen months. Then she had stopped. She said that she had quit because she no longer needed to keep the journal. She was living in a continuous state of gratitude.

I asked to know more. She indicated that her father was a very critical man and she had acquired this same trait. If she heard a wonderful concert but the soloist missed a note, she remembered the mistake rather than the beautiful music that surrounded it. She related to people in a similar fashion. Rather than celebrating their gifts and what they did right she looked for their flaws; she was even constantly trying to correct her loved ones. The quality of her life reflected her focus. Because she focused on the negative, what she saw inside herself and all around her were the flaws and the problems.

Schon's story is important. It seems that she had rewired her own brain. But how?

At first, Schon struggled to find three positive things to write in her gratitude journal each day. But soon she experienced the rewards intrinsic to gratitude. Living in a state of gratitude increased her desire to live in gratitude and made it easier to feel grateful. She extended her efforts. While continuing to write in her journal, she asked her family to share three expressions of gratitude with each other at dinner every night. Her life became increasingly happy as her family became more focused on the gifts of the day, caring more about each other's successes than failures. In becoming more grateful, Schon greatly increased her positivity ratio. She had become a new person.

I was so impressed with this account that the next day I started keeping a gratitude journal. Each morning I would write these words: "Today I am grateful for ____." I would then examine the previous day and write. Within just a few days, I began to notice a very big difference. For one thing, I noticed that my ability to make mental associations skyrocketed. At dinner with some old friends, I began talking like crazy and really enjoying it, although I am normally somewhat reserved in conversation. It was shocking to see this change in myself.

A dinner conversation may seem like a trivial illustration. What is important is the increase in mental associations that made my unusual willingness to participate in the conversation possible. Creative thinking is about combining unlike things. At that meal I was creating generative conversation. But I was not only having this experience in restaurants. I was having it everywhere I went. My positivity ratio was soaring, causing me to interact with the world in new ways.

As I continued to change, I decided to make myself accountable. I told twelve family members that I would send them my daily entry in my gratitude journal. They were not expected to respond. I just wanted to share. Soon several members of my family began to keep gratitude journals. They also began to report personal changes.

As happened to Kathy, the personal changes did not end at home. We also take our increased positivity to work. Two of my children who started to keep gratitude journals reported that they had asked their colleagues to join them in various gratitude exercises, with tangible results. I began to share these results in public presentations. Many people in my audiences now make the decision to keep a gratitude journal and later contact me to share stories of personal change. The ripple effect has been continuous.

Think About It

- How did you feel when you read Kathy's and Schon's stories about keeping a gratitude journal? About sharing their journal entries with others?

  _____

  _____

  _____

- How would you feel about starting a gratitude journal of your own? Do you think it would be difficult to think of three things to be grateful for every single day? If so, why?

  _____

  _____

  _____

- Do you think that asking your staff to keep gratitude journals would be a useful way to increase positivity in your organization? Would you expect them to resist? Why? How would you attract them into transcending their natural resistance to your suggestion?

  _____

  _____

  _____

THE POWER OF THE POSITIVE

The power of gratitude journals in increasing positivity made me more aware of the importance of emotions in learning. As I watched Kathy's presentation and thought about my own presentation, I could feel myself becoming more open to possibilities and more attuned to the audience's needs. I again asked myself the questions listed earlier: What result do I want to create? Am I internally directed? Am I other-focused? Am I externally open?

Walking to the stage, I suddenly knew what to do. Out of my mouth came words that emerged in the very moment: "Please tell me what you felt when Kathy spoke."

This question surprised the audience. It was not the start they expected. They were silent for a few moments. Finally they started giving intellectual responses. I pointed out that their answers did not address my question; I had asked about their feelings. I asked them to try once more. This caused a discernible change. The answers were more personal, honest, and authentic. Several people indicated that they felt inspired by what Kathy had done. The climate changed. The entire audience began moving toward a more positive emotional state.

I then frankly described the fears I had experienced a few minutes earlier and how negative emotions had been closing me down. This personal, honest, and authentic statement also surprised them. I could feel them responding to my authenticity. I could feel them supporting me.

I told them that Kathy's genuine expressions stimulated courage in me. I told them how I had experienced a flood of new thoughts, among them the intuition that I should start my presentation with the question about Kathy's story. I said I was now standing before them with great confidence about the day to come. I was confident that they would elevate their lives and elevate the school.

Then I said, "Over the last year Kathy had the courage to apply what she learned. She has become a more effective version of herself. Today, she had the courage to be authentic, and she has lifted many people in the room—including me. Kathy is a staff person; she is also a positive leader. Today, she led this entire organization. By taking us into the positive emotional realm, she increased our ability to perform. Leadership is influence, and influence is not determined by hierarchical position."

This was another significant moment. Although the statement ran counter to normal expectations, everyone recognized that it was true. They could see that anyone—even a low-ranking "staff person"—can change the people in an organization. In that moment, the audience experienced a paradigm shift. Their feelings and thoughts became more positive, and they became open to possibility.

In the day's final exercise, the audience enthusiastically filled a whiteboard with compelling ideas on how the school could become more positive and effective. They were able to do that because they had moved out of their normal state and into an elevated state. With inspiration from Kathy and a few nudges from me, they were able to move forward in a state of shared leadership. They were able to move past the conflict that was holding them back. They were able to engage in spontaneous, creative, and productive conversation, and new organizing images were beginning to emerge.

Think About It

- Why did the right question suddenly come into my mind?

_____

_____

_____

- Why did the audience respond to my authenticity?

_____

_____

_____

- Why did the audience have so many ideas in the final exercise?

_____

_____

_____

- What are the general principles you derive from this story?

_____

_____

_____

Personal Reflection and Application

REFLECT

While the chapter is fresh in your mind, quickly write down the 4 to 6 points, concepts, or ideas that stand out for you the most.

_____

_____

_____

WATCH THE FILM: *GANDHI*

In this film, a man transforms the policies of one country and the government of another. From Gandhi's story, we can learn much about the fundamental state of leadership and the process of deep change.

Questions to Consider

1. Think about Gandhi's experiences in South Africa.

    • What was his leadership challenge in South Africa?

    _____

    _____

    _____

    • What events most contributed to his development as a leader?

    _____

    _____

    _____

    • What did you learn from his initial walk with Charlie Andrews? From the pass-burning incident?

    _____

    _____

    _____

- Why was he successful in South Africa?

  _____

  _____

  _____

  _____

- In what ways are his experiences relevant to your own development as a leader?

  _____

  _____

  _____

  _____

2. Gandhi had a vision and a strategy for changing India.

   - What was his vision? His strategy?

     _____

     _____

     _____

     _____

   - How did his vision and strategy originate and evolve?

     _____

     _____

     _____

     _____

   - What is your own vision and strategy? How did they originate and how are they evolving?

     _____

     _____

     _____

     _____

3. Gandhi seems to transcend normal assumptions.

    •   What positive assumptions did Gandhi tend to make?

    _____

    _____

    _____

    _____

    •   What were his most counterintuitive moves? Why did he make them?

    _____

    _____

    _____

    _____

    •   When have you made counterintuitive leadership moves? Why did you make them?

    _____

    _____

    _____

    _____

4. At a dark moment, in prison, Gandhi converses with a photographer from *Life Magazine.*

    •   What does this conversation teach you about Gandhi's orientation to positivity?

    _____

    _____

    _____

    _____

- How did Gandhi's positivity help him succeed?

_____

_____

_____

5. Gandhi said that he was in control. But his opponent was the entire British Empire.

- What made Gandhi think that he was in control when his opponent was so powerful?

_____

_____

_____

- How could you access the kind of power that Gandhi acquired?

_____

_____

_____

- Do you think that Gandhi continued to change after he was put in prison?

_____

_____

_____

- Why couldn't the British answer the question, "Who is leading them?"

_____

_____

_____

- Who *was* leading them? How was this possible? What does it have to do with the notion of an organizing image as discussed in this chapter?

_____

_____

_____

6. If Gandhi were invited to speak to three hundred business leaders in a country on the verge of collapse, what might he say?

_____

_____

_____

7. Which of Gandhi's behaviors best indicates that he was results-centered? Internally directed? Other-focused? Externally open?

_____

_____

_____

8. List your key insights about leadership and positivity from the film and briefly describe some life experiences that you associate with these insights.

_____

_____

_____

MAKE A JOURNAL ENTRY

Read the following statements. Check the 2 or 3 that resonate most with you.

___1. Lacking hope that others will change and not trusting others to do their part, everyone pursues his or her own personal good.

___2. Every organization, group, and relationship is subject to the tyranny of self-interest.

___3. "Do I ever contribute to the corruption of the collective?"

___4. Real leadership is pursuing the common good of the system.

___5. Positive emotions improve our ability to cope with adversity and increase the likelihood of finding positive meaning in what is going on around us, even when we are surrounded by negative processes.

___6. I, like so many others, tend to avoid self-change.

___7. "Today, she had the courage to be authentic, and she has lifted many people in the room—including me."

___8. Leadership is influence and influence is not determined by hierarchical position.

Now circle the number of the single statement you most resonate with. List some life experiences that you associate with that statement. Then write a paragraph that expresses the importance of one of those life experiences.

Life experiences:

_____

_____

_____

Paragraph:

_____

_____

_____

WRITE A MEMO

Based on your insights, your responses to the questions about the film, and your journal entry, write a short note to someone you know explaining the essence of what you have learned in this chapter.

_____

_____

_____

_____

_____

APPLY THE LEARNING

What are one or two actions you will take from what you have learned in this chapter to continue your journey toward mastery of the deep change process?

_____

_____

_____

_____

_____

CHAPTER EIGHT

INVITING OTHERS TO DEEP CHANGE

IN THIS CHAPTER

- Leaders and teachers have the same task. It is to transform their followers through the use of moral power. We can learn leadership by pondering great teaching.

- Teachers in the fundamental state of leadership invite others to transcend the ordinary and recognize their own greatness. They become leaders.

- Normal teachers of leadership propound theories, analyze cases, and seek to develop skills. They do not create crucibles of character development.

- Great teachers turn secular conversations into sacred conversations. When we participate in those conversations, we feel our consciousness expand and we gain faith in our own potential.

The concept of the fundamental state of leadership changes how we think about leadership and the way leaders develop. Leadership is not authority but influence. Everyone has influence, whether positive or negative. The psychological state we are in determines the quality of influence we exert. If we are in the normal state—comfort-centered, externally directed, self-focused, or internally closed—we can elevate ourselves to a fundamental state of leadership by choosing to be purpose-centered, internally directed, other-focused, and externally open. When we choose to enter the fundamental state of leadership, we are more likely to attract others into that state. We can then attract those people from patterns of normal organizing to patterns of positive organizing.

In this chapter we consider how to invite others to begin the deep change process. By now, it should be clear that the first requirement is to have entered the fundamental state of leadership ourselves. There is no way to "teach" what it means to be a leader except by *being* what we wish to invoke in others.

Here we encounter a difficulty. The fundamental state of leadership is fragile. It is difficult to get ourselves into that state and even harder to stay in it once we enter.

THE EPISODIC NATURE OF THE FUNDAMENTAL STATE OF LEADERSHIP

When we leave that state in which we are purpose-centered and internally directed, other-focused, and externally open, we have to make the choice to return. That said, if we have entered the fundamental state of leadership once, we know the path that will lead us back to it in the future.

One of my students, Jeremy, put it this way:

I have little doubt that I will face many more perspective changes in the time left to me in this life. Although I can't honestly say that I look forward to the paralysis and fear of "walking naked into uncertainty" that precedes my own shifts in paradigm, I have come to realize the great value of moving through in order to embrace my own emerging deep change reality. I recently found an executive coach skilled in appreciative inquiry to help me face my moments of illusion, panic, exhaustion, and stagnation—moments of slow death and failure to stay in the transformative cycle.

Jeremy understands that we move into and out of the fundamental state of leadership. He has also come to value being in the fundamental state of leadership so highly that he sought someone to help him face his fears. Most people are not like Jeremy. When I ask them to tell me of the great moments in their life, they often respond in a recognizable pattern. First they tell me they faced a very difficult challenge. Then they tell me a story of courage, persistence, and triumph. They describe how much they learned, even from unwanted experiences. They speak of the event as a peak experience. Then they say, "But I would never want to do that again." This is a telling refrain that illustrates the high cost of growth, and our natural tendency to scamper back into our comfort zones.

Think About It

- When have you "walked naked into uncertainty?" What happened afterward? Did you seek out new challenges? Or did you think, "I never want to do that again!" Why?

_____

_____

_____

WALKING NAKED INTO THE LAND OF UNCERTAINTY — AGAIN

Some people, like Jeremy, learn the value of being in the fundamental state of leadership and work to be there regularly. Knowing that they have been in an extraordinary state previously helps them move forward in the present. Tom Glocer is such a man. In my book _Building the Bridge As You Walk On It_ (2010), he tells an important story:

Tom was a young lawyer at Reuters. At the time, Reuters was making profits in every country where it operated except Brazil. Tom was offered a line management job leading the Brazilian operation.

In an attempt to reduce Tom's anxiety, the CEO told Tom that Brazil had been a problem for a long time and that it was unlikely he could actually turn it around. Tom saw this as a challenge. He prepared for his new assignment by gathering information, analyzing trends, and planning ways to improve the Brazilian operation.

When he arrived in Brazil, it took only a half day to discover that the operation was totally corrupt. Incompetence, cronyism, and outright theft were rampant. Managers from other countries were counting the days until they could leave. The operation was hopeless.

By noon of his first day Tom made a fundamental decision. He threw out all his analysis and plans. Instead, he decided to fire all but three people and rebuild the entire organization, even though he had no experience leading such a change. He says, "I was not a surgeon, but the patient was going to die." Like a doctor in a crisis, he began to move forward, choosing to make complicated decisions despite having insufficient information. He was truly building the bridge as he walked on it. He left behind the systematic mind of the lawyer and walked naked into the land of uncertainty. His efforts eventually succeeded, and Brazil became a profitable operation.

Here is how Tom looks back on that experience:

> There was so much urgency. I had no choice. I had to act. If something blew up, it did not matter. Things were so bad there was only one way to go. So I did what I had to do. It was terrifying, but we learned how to do what needed to be done. It was the best work I have ever done. (pp. 218–220)

A few years later, Tom would once again face what seemed to be an impossible challenge. By then, Reuters had shared the fate of many information companies in the post-dot-com era, and its shares had lost 90 percent of their value. The new CEO, the man responsible for the life or death of the company, was Tom Glocer. Once again, Tom was walking naked into the land of uncertainty. In the middle of the journey he wrote:

> I am struck by stories of managers who, whatever their level, move themselves beyond fear or self-preservation to act with true and decisive freedom. Once so liberated their power knows no limits and with it, their value to their companies soars.
>
> Despite the heroism of so many of the personal and corporate stories of growth related in cases of deep change, the striking feature for me is that they are *told in retrospect*. I do not say this to demean the power or pathos of the personal journeys recounted, but rather to highlight my own discomfort at telling my story before I know the ending.

Reuters is my company. It is a 152-year-old institution I deeply love and one which the world would be poorer without. I have launched it into a transformation which employees, investors, and customers find threatening. I am calmly confident, however, that there is no other path.

We at Reuters have been through a wretched time in the eyes of market analysts and the UK media. Out of their pessimism, however, has ironically grown a great freedom for me which I have known only once before in my career. I can do no wrong—and hence I can do great good—because I am free of the incrementalism born of mediocre success.

I do not know how this story will end, but I could not care more, work harder, or fear less. To me these are the seeds of success.

We now know that the story turned out very well. The transformation was successful. Reuters and Thomson eventually merged and Tom was appointed CEO. But even if the episode had been unsuccessful—and some efforts at deep change are unsuccessful—the story is inherently instructive.

Note that in the middle of the chaos, Tom was doing what he had to do in order to meet his greatest responsibility: he was moving forward through the uncertainty of transformation, putting the corporate good ahead of his own. All of this was a little easier because of what he had done in Brazil; he had been in the fundamental state of leadership before.

Think About It

Tom says, "I do not know how this story will end, but I could not care more, work harder, or fear less. To me these are the seeds of success."

- What do you think Tom meant by that statement?

_____

_____

_____

_____

_____

- Can you imagine making that statement yourself? Under what circumstances?

_____

_____

_____

LESSONS FOR TRANSFORMATIONAL TEACHERS

Tom's story provides important lessons to those who would invite others into the fundamental state of leadership. First, just as a great artist does not remain in a continual state of peak inspiration and creativity, we do not remain continually in the fundamental state. Second, each time we are required to enter the fundamental state of leadership it is a new challenge. We must meet and conquer new fears and overcome once again those that we faced in the past. Third, each time we enter the fundamental state of leadership, we acquire learning and confidence that make that state more accessible to us in the future. The learning necessary to successful transformation requires someone, like Tom, to exercise the courage to put the collective interest ahead of personal survival. That courage can then spread to the other members of the collective. Organizational transformation is about increased collective virtue. A transformational leader works to constantly increase the integrity of both the self and the organization.

The preceding reflections have important implications for how we go about educating and developing leaders. Few institutions are able to turn managers into leaders, because those who teach leadership rarely stray outside their zone of comfort or ask their students to do so. The classrooms of such teachers are organizations designed on normal assumptions. These teachers call attention to leaders who produce positive organizing, but the teachers model a path that leads elsewhere. Normal teachers may share theories of leadership, analyze cases, and seek to develop skills, but they do not create crucibles of character development.

Transformational teaching is about attracting people to decide to enter the unique state from which their own great thinking and great behaviors can emanate. This happens only when the teacher chooses to become more purpose-centered, internally directed, other-focused, and externally open. In other words, you can only develop leaders by being a leader. Great teaching is great leadership, which gives rise to great relationships.

Think of Gail's story in Chapter Six. As she entered the fundamental state of leadership and became more purposeful, authentic, concerned, and open, her clients flourished. As a therapist she became a great leader and a great teacher. The changes in her increased the quality of her relationships, and other people were thus better able to transform themselves.

The objective of leadership development efforts should be to attract people to enter the fundamental state of leadership more often and increase the duration of the time they spend in it. To achieve this, instructors have to transcend the assumptions of normal organizing and administrators have to accept programs with greater authenticity and risk. In the following sections, we will meet two people who exemplify this style of leadership development.

Think About It

- Have you been involved in a program that followed the normal ways of teaching leadership? What were the results? How well was the program able to transform managers into leaders?

  _____

  _____

  _____

  _____

- Have you ever had a teacher, or perhaps a mentor like Reuben in *Norma Rae*, who was able to attract you into the fundamental state of leadership? What did that person do?

  _____

  _____

  _____

  _____

CREATING SACRED SPACE

Larry Peters is a professor at Texas Christian University who has had substantial experience helping both executives and students enter the fundamental state of leadership. Here is what Larry has to say about leadership (Quinn, 2004, pp. 222–224).

I have spent considerable time consulting with senior executives and managers who seemed to view change as a detached, third party management task, but with bigger aspirations. Their message seemed to say that change was necessary for everyone but themselves—"Change you . . . but leave me unchanged!" I would confront them about the lack of commitment I saw and heard . . . in their personal stories of why their behavior did not reflect the action, passion, or commitment of a real leader.

What I heard was that it was too dangerous to really lead in the highly political world they lived in. In fact, every instance of failed leadership seemed to reflect a concern for personal (i.e., job and career) safety.

How can one lead others to more effective solutions if one is not willing to challenge the foundations of the dysfunctional world that produced less than effective results?

We can't unless we experience profound change, transformational change . . . deep change. We need to care more about what is right, what is effective, what is moral, and what can't be denied any longer, than we [care] about our personal well-being. We need to step out of the transactional reality we seem trapped in to find something worth "dying for"—and worth living for!

That is the essence of leadership. It's passion and commitment for a cause. It's caring more about one's mission or vision or people or justice than about one's self. Process models of leadership can only produce results if enacted by leaders. Detached, third-person leadership, no matter how well it follows the sage advice of those who teach "how to lead," does not produce the results we want and need. *It's not the mechanics, it's the person!*

Larry's insights suggested a way of teaching that would allow the people he was working with to connect with the message in a deep way. He goes on to explain what he does:

I recently shared this message in an executive MBA course on leadership. My students shared many examples of failed leadership, from those who settled for "peace and pay" to those who tried to "manage" people to a new future. I had my students think about deep change that they experienced in their lives (or that others close to them experienced) and had them share stories with the class.

We heard stories of a man who lost a child in a car accident (and who changed the seat belt law in Texas); a woman who was promoted to the toughest assignment in her company, a position for which she had no prior training; and a man who was given the assignment of opening a market in China and found everything he knew about management didn't work. We heard stories of passion and focus and courage and commitment and perseverance and energy. We heard stories that produced results beyond anyone's expectations, and we saw the emotion and shared the feelings of pride these people had. We saw what was possible when people experienced deep change. Nobody in that room will ever mistake management for true leadership again. They raised the bar on themselves that afternoon—and on everyone else who presumes to lead.

Change me first! The message is so simple, so powerful.

Larry is no ordinary teacher. He not only recognizes the hypocrisy in executives' normal language, the way they allocate time, and their personal stories, but also challenges it. He understands that we enter the fundamental state of leadership when we decide to. The problem is that because so many people want to believe that they bear no responsibility, it is almost impossible to teach them that they do. Remember Andrea's refrain in *The Devil Wears Prada:* "I had no choice." People have numerous defense mechanisms that automatically kick in when they are taught ideas like these. So how does Larry teach people who do not want to learn this lesson?

Larry does something brilliant: instead of playing the role of expert, he asks his students, "Can you identify deep change experiences in your lives or the lives of other people whom you know?" By asking people to share their stories instead of telling them what to do, Larry transforms the classroom from a profane space to a sacred space.

What does this mean? A sacred space is a place where people can share their most authentic feelings and thoughts. In authentic conversations, trust grows. The group pays attention, adapts, learns, discovers, and generates knowledge. When we participate in such a group, we feel consciousness expand and gain more faith in our own potential.

Think About It

- Have you ever been in the kind of authentic conversation that Larry described? At the time, were you and others operating under normal assumptions or the assumptions of positive organizing?

_____

_____

_____

- How do you, as a leader, bring about such a conversation? List some guidelines.

_____

_____

_____

BECOMING A MORE TRANSFORMATIONAL TEACHER

We do not know for sure how Larry became a teacher who could develop transformational leaders. But we can gain some insight from Doug Anderson, who shares his own story of becoming a transformational teacher.

After teaching business strategy at Harvard, Doug helped build a major business that provided educational programs in many of the world's largest companies. He then became dean of the Huntsman School of Business at Utah State University. In that position he has been successful in moving the institution forward. His story is not unlike those that were shared in Larry's classroom (Quinn, 2004, pp. 225–227):

> I have often heard it said that "you never really learn a thing until you teach it to someone else." And it is true—there is a powerful connection between teaching and learning. [To me] teaching seemed like a great way to continue learning. But it is not the only way, and maybe not the most powerful way—there is also the learning that comes from applying or experiencing an idea.
>
> I was a member of a consulting team that was using the concepts of *Deep Change* to help a major utility transform itself from an engineering-driven company to one that was much more focused on market and competitive realities. From the outset, I expected this to be a fascinating intellectual journey. It turned out to be far more than that. It became personal.
>
> During much of the decade of the 1990s my first marriage was slowly dying. I knew my wife was not happy, but I always believed we would get through it. Sometimes she'd try to talk about divorce, but I wouldn't consider it. When you are rafting down the Colorado River and encounter white water, I'd say, that's not the time to jump out, or to push your partner out. I was sure there would be calm water ahead.
>
> She didn't believe it. In May 1998 the perfect storm hit. I had planned a three-day business trip to Houston to coincide with the anniversary of [my brother's] death. At noon on the day I was to leave, there came a knock on the door. I answered to find an officer of the court, with divorce papers in hand. "Your court appearance is scheduled for the day after tomorrow," he said.
>
> I was stunned. But I couldn't see an option for canceling my client engagement. Obviously, I would not be able to represent myself in court. I called an attorney friend and spent the afternoon with him, [arriving] at the client's conference center well after midnight. The next morning at eight o'clock I opened a three-day seminar. At the end of the three days, I visited my sister-in-law [who had lost her husband]. Instead of comforting her, I collapsed.
>
> The divorce took two years to become final. I was powerless to prevent it. As I spun through the grief cycle, I found myself returning again

and again to the concepts in *Deep Change*. I had never experienced this kind of sorrow before. *Deep Change* became a mirror for me. I was not always comfortable with what I saw. I began to recognize integrity gaps that I had not previously acknowledged.

My teaching became much more personal. In each session, as I challenged participants to confront their integrity gaps, I challenged myself. And, as I acted on those commitments, a new self emerged, a learner who was now a much better guide to others on journeys of discovery and transformation.

In the hero's journey, the hero sets out on a quest and, before returning to his home community as an "empowered and empowering" leader, must slay the beast. The beast he slays is his old self. That's what deep change is all about: the renewal and the replenishment of self and the enlargement of others.

Doug observed that the most powerful education comes from the experience of applying ideas and experiencing the consequences. I was moved when he said, "I had never experienced this kind of sorrow." When we have such feelings, we are forced to work in a way we would never have worked when we were in the normal state.

As Doug moved into the fundamental state of leadership, he began to redefine who he was. He saw what he would normally deny. His teaching became more personal. He challenged his students to close their integrity gaps while he was striving to close his own. At that point he was teaching with increased moral power. As he did such teaching, Doug continued to grow. He became more purpose-centered and other-focused, more internally directed and externally open. He began to attract others into the fundamental state of leadership.

Think About It

- What might be some reasons why Doug's grief led him to the concepts in *Deep Change*? Why wasn't he able to change himself before the divorce?

_____

_____

_____

- How are the outcomes of Doug's story like the outcomes of Gail's story in Chapter Six? Given the differences in the stories, why are the outcomes similar?

  _____

  _____

  _____

- As you think of the stories of Doug and Gail, what episode of your life comes to mind? What happened as a result?

  _____

  _____

  _____

ATTRACTING OTHERS INTO THE FUNDAMENTAL STATE OF LEADERSHIP

We have seen that leadership development, like organizational transformation, begins with personal change. We learn from Tom the episodic nature of the fundamental state of leadership. Each entry into the fundamental state of leadership is both terrifying and exhilarating, and while we are on the journey of deep change no insurance policy guarantees success. We do not know how the story will end. We learn from Larry's students that ordinary people—the people sitting next to us—have a history of such experiences. We learn from Larry that it is possible to create sacred space, and that in sacred space the characteristics that invite people into the fundamental state of leadership naturally emerge. We learn from Doug that teachers are human beings who must face the challenge of deep change. His example is proof that the willingness to face deep change alters how we think about developing others. Once we are willing to change, we begin to let go of telling and forcing. We begin to turn to transcending self and participating with others in the creation of sacred space. As we do so we grow and they grow.

In the end Tom, Larry, and Doug teach us that we are all both ordinary and magnificent. We are all drawn to live in the normal state, and we all tend to move toward personal entropy and slow death. The challenge is to make deep change and enter the creative state, to live in ever-increasing integrity. When we choose deep change we enter the fundamental state of leadership. In that state we experience exponential growth, and we become living attractors, pulling some of those around us into the same state. With those people we create sacred space and engage in a social movement. As more and more of us accept the invitation to transform ourselves, we become a productive community continually striving to adapt to emerging reality. Together, we build the bridge as we walk on it.

Personal Reflection and Application

REFLECT

While the chapter is fresh in your mind, quickly write down the 4 to 6 points, concepts, or ideas that stand out for you the most.

_____

_____

_____

WATCH THE FILM: *DEAD POETS SOCIETY*

This film is an account of life in a boarding school for wealthy students. The culture of the school is based on hierarchical assumptions, and the teachers tend to be didactic. The boys are socialized to embrace traditional aspirations and to make normal assumptions about how to move forward in their lives.

One day, a new teacher, Mr. Keating, arrives. Mr. Keating relates to the boys as people and seeks to inspire them to think for themselves. We watch as he provides transformational leadership and develops a new culture.

Questions to Consider

In an early scene we see teachers introducing classes in science, languages, and mathematics.

- What do the teachers' approaches have in common?

  _____

  _____

  _____

  _____

- How does Mr. Keating's approach contrast with the others? What does this tell you about him?

  _____

  _____

  _____

  _____

- How do the boys react to Mr. Keating's approach?

  _____

  _____

  _____

  _____

1. At dinner, Mr. McAllister, another teacher, tells Mr. Keating, "You take a big risk by encouraging them to be artists, John. When they realize they're not Rembrandts, Shakespeares, or Mozarts, they'll hate you for it."

- What does Mr. McAllister mean?

  _____

  _____

  _____

  _____

- What is right about his argument?

  _____

  _____

  _____

  _____

- How could this argument be reversed to condemn a teacher who does not encourage students to search out their greatest potential?

  _____

  _____

  _____

  _____

2. Mr. Keating quotes Henry David Thoreau: "I went to the woods because I wanted to live deliberately. I wanted to live deep and suck out all the marrow of life." Escalante in *Stand and Deliver* (Chapter Six) made a similar statement about desire. What does desire and the creation of desire have to do with leadership?

  _____

  _____

  _____

  _____

3. Mr. Keating stands up on his desk to "remind myself that we must constantly look at things in a different way" and asks the boys to "break out."

- What does looking at things from a different way have to do with leadership?

  _____

  _____

  _____

  _____

- What does it mean for someone to break out?

  _____

  _____

  _____

  _____

4. Mr. Keating also tells the boys that they need to strive to find their own voice. Later, one of the boys, Todd, tells another, "You say things and people listen. I am not like that."

- How is Todd like the prince in *The King's Speech*?

  _____

  _____

  _____

  _____

- What happens when a person with no voice is placed in a position of authority?

  _____

  _____

  _____

  _____

- What happens when a leader's followers have no voice?

  _____

  _____

  _____

  _____

- How does a leader help someone develop their voice?

  _____

  _____

  _____

  _____

5. When Todd does not do the poetry assignment, Mr. Keating calls him up to the front of the class and walks him through the development of a poem. When he is finished, the class bursts into applause.

- How did Mr. Keating know to use this particular approach to help Todd find his voice? Was it in his teaching plan?

_____

_____

_____

- Why was this moment a personal transformation for Todd?

_____

_____

_____

- How is Todd's transformation like that of Norma in *Norma Rae*, the students in *Stand and Deliver*, and the prince in *The King's Speech*?

_____

_____

_____

- What are the implications of this scene for a leader?

_____

_____

_____

6. After a student, Knox, publishes an article in the school paper, the headmaster, Mr. Nolan, tells Mr. Keating that the school's curriculum is designed to establish tradition and discipline, not to encourage the students to think for themselves.

- What does Mr. Nolan's statement tell you about the organization?

_____

_____

_____

- Does the school's organization resemble other organizations you have known? In what ways?

  _____

  _____

  _____

7. Mr. Keating tells Neil that he loves teaching and doesn't want to be anywhere else.
   - What role did this kind of love play in the lives of Reuben in _Norma Rae,_ Escalante in _Stand and Deliver,_ and Lionel in _The King's Speech?_

     _____

     _____

     _____

     _____

   - Why is Mr. Keating's statement relevant to a leader?

     _____

     _____

     _____

     _____

8. Mr. Nolan blames Mr. Keating for encouraging the "reckless and self-indulgent behavior" that led to Neil Perry's death.
   - Was Mr. Nolan right? Did Mr. Keating abuse his position, and was he responsible for Neil's death? Why or why not?

     _____

     _____

     _____

     _____

- What does this scene tell you about what can happen to leaders?

  _____

  _____

  _____

9. In the last scene, the boys stand on their desks and address Mr. Keating as he leaves. Why? What is the significance of this act?

    _____

    _____

    _____

10. List the key insights you gained from the film about inviting others to deep change and briefly describe some life experiences that you associate with these insights.

    _____

    _____

    _____

MAKE A JOURNAL ENTRY

Following are several quotes from the chapter. Check the 2 or 3 quotes that resonate most with you.

___1. There is no way to "teach" what it means to be a leader except by *being* what we wish to invoke in others.

___2. Transformational teaching is about attracting people to decide to enter the unique state from which their own great thinking and great behaviors can emanate.

___3. "I have come to realize the great value of moving through paralysis and fear in order to embrace my own emerging deep change reality."

___4. A transformational leader works to constantly increase the integrity of both the self and the organization.

___5. "Their message seemed to say that change was necessary for everyone but themselves—'Change you . . . but leave me unchanged!'"

___6. How can one lead others to more effective solutions if one is not willing to challenge the foundations of the dysfunctional world that produced less than effective results?

___7. By asking people to share their stories instead of telling them what to do, Larry transforms the classroom from a profane space to a sacred space.

___8. "*Deep Change* became a mirror for me. I was not always comfortable with what I saw."

___9. Once we are willing to change, we begin to let go of telling and forcing.

___10. Tom, Larry, and Doug teach us that we are all both ordinary and magnificent.

___11. When we choose deep change we enter the fundamental state of leadership.

Now circle the number of the single statement you most resonate with. List some life experiences that you associate with that statement. Then write a paragraph that expresses the importance of one of those life experiences.

Life experiences:

_____

_____

_____

Paragraph:

_____

_____

_____

WRITE A MEMO

Based on your insights, your responses to the questions about the film, and your journal entry, write a short note to someone you know. Help the person understand the essence of what you have learned in this chapter.

_____

_____

_____

_____

_____

APPLY THE LEARNING

What are one or two actions you will take to use what you have learned about deep change to improve leadership development in your organization?

_____

_____

_____

_____

_____

PUT THE LEARNING TO WORK

Now it's time to pull together what you have learned from this field guide about the process of deep change and about yourself. The following questions will help you focus on how you will use that learning to improve your life and your organization.

1. Imagine that you are going to give a talk on deep change to a group of executives. What are the most important things you will tell them? Briefly describe each of those key points.

   _____

   _____

   _____

2. What are the most important insights you have had about yourself? Briefly describe them.

   _____

   _____

   _____

3. Think about what it means to be able to put yourself in a fundamental state of leadership. How can you use the four dimensions to more regularly put yourself in this state?

Purpose-centered:

_____

_____

_____

Internally directed:

_____

_____

_____

Other-focused:

_____

_____

_____

Externally open:

_____

_____

_____

4. What is your life mission? Why are you on this planet?

_____

_____

_____

_____

My one-sentence life mission is:

_____

_____

_____

5. Thinking about changes you would like to make on your journey toward mastery of deep change, what are your 1 to 3 most important goals for the next 1 to 3 months? What will you do to achieve each goal? How will you know when you have achieved it?

    Goal #1:

    _____

    _____

    _____

    _____

    _____

    _____

    Goal #2:

    _____

    _____

    _____

    _____

    _____

    _____

    Goal #3:

    _____

    _____

    _____

    _____

    _____

    _____

CONTINUING YOUR JOURNEY

This is a message of thanks to you, the reader.

In my nearly thirty-five years of teaching, training, speaking, and consulting, I have come to deeply respect the effort it takes to pursue deep change. It requires the courage to embrace purpose, integrity, empathy, and learning. When people make this choice, good things happen and positive influence spreads. The world becomes a better place and we are all, in some way, enlarged. So I thank you for going through this field guide, for taking the time and making the effort to learn and apply these concepts. And I wish you well on your continuing journey toward the mastery of deep change.

SHARE YOUR INSIGHTS

As you have gone through this field guide, you have learned through the stories told by others who have embarked on the journey of deep change. If you have an insight or a meaningful story about deep change that you would like to share, please send it to me at requinn@umich.edu. Appropriate submissions will be posted on our website: http://www.leadingwithlift.com/blog/

READINGS AND RESOURCES

If you would like to learn more about the deep change process, we suggest the following books:

By the author: *Deep Change* (1996); *Change the World* (2000); *Building the Bridge As You Walk On It* (2004); *Lift: Becoming a Positive Force in Any Situation* (2009).

By others: *Path of Least Resistance: Learning to Become the Creative Force in Your Own Life*, Robert Fritz; *Mindset: The New Psychology of Success*, Carol Dweck; *Positivity: Top-Notch Research Reveals the 3 to 1 Ratio That Will Change Your Life*, Barbara Frederickson; *Leadership and Self-Deception: Getting out of the Box*, The Arbinger Institute; *The Power of a Positive No*, William Ury; *Positive Leadership: Strategies for Extraordinary Performance*, Kim S. Cameron; *The Power of Full Engagement*, Jim Loehr and Tony Schwartz; *Managing Transitions: Making the Most of Change*, William Bridges and Susan Bridges; *True North*, Bill George and Peter Sims; *Flourish: A Visionary New Understanding of Happiness and Well-Being*, Martin Seligman; *Flow: The Psychology of Optimal Experience*, Mihaly Csikszentmihalyi; *Leading Change*, John Kotter; *Leadership Without Easy Answers*, Ronald Heifetz; *Theory U: Leading from the Future As It Emerges*, Otto Scharmer; *Leadership from the Inside Out: Becoming a Leader for Life*, Kevin Cashman; *Immunity to Change*, Robert Kegan and Lisa Laskow Lahey.

BIBLIOGRAPHY

Avolio, Bruce, and Hannah, Sean. "Developmental Readiness: Accelerating Leader Development." *Consulting Psychology Journal: Practice and Research*, 2008, *60*(4), 331−347.

"Avon's Andrea Jung: CEOs Need to Reinvent Themselves." *USA Today*, June 14, 2009. http://www.usatoday.com/money/companies/management/advice/2009-06-14-jung -ceo-avon_N.htm

Cameron, Kim S., and Quinn, Robert. *Diagnosing and Changing Organizational Culture*. San Francisco: Jossey-Bass, 2011.

Csikszentmihalyi, Mihaly. *Creativity: Flow and the Psychology of Discovery and Invention*. New York: HarperCollins, 1997.

Fredrickson, Barbara. *Positivity*. New York: Three Rivers Press, 2009.

Fritz, Robert. *The Path of Least Resistance: Learning to Become the Creative Force in Your Own Life*. New York: Fawcett Columbine, 1989.

Kazin, Alfred. (ed.). *The Portable Blake.* "All Are Men in Eternity. " [From *Jerusalem.*] New York: Viking Penguin, 1974.

Mandela, Nelson. *Long Walk to Freedom.* London: Abacus/Little, Brown, 1994.

Niederhoffer, Kate, and Pennebaker, James. "Sharing One's Own Story: On the Benefits of Writing or Talking About Emotional Experience." In C. R. Snyder and Shane J. Lopez (eds.), *Handbook of Positive Psychology.* New York: Oxford University Press, 2002.

Pirsig, Robert. *Zen and the Art of Motorcycle Maintenance.* New York: William Morrow, 1974.

Quinn, Robert. *Deep Change: Discovering the Leader Within.* San Francisco: Jossey-Bass, 1996.

Quinn, Robert. *Change the World: How Ordinary People Can Accomplish Extraordinary Results.* San Francisco: Jossey-Bass, 2000.

Quinn, Robert. *Building the Bridge As You Walk On It: A Guide for Leading Change.* San Francisco: Jossey-Bass, 2004.

Quinn, Robert, and Quinn, Ryan. *Lift: Becoming a Positive Force in Any Situation.* San Francisco: Berrett-Koehler, 2009.

Quinn, Robert, and Spreitzer, Gretchen. "The Psychometrics of the Competing Values Culture Instrument and an Analysis of the Impact of Organizational Culture on Quality of Life." *Research in Organizational Change and Development,* 1991, *5,* 115–142.

Roberts, Monty. *The Man Who Listens to Horses.* New York: Random House, 1997.

Scharmer, Otto. *Theory U: Leading from the Future As It Emerges.* San Francisco: Berrett-Koehler, 2009.

Thoreau, Henry David. "On the Duty of Civil Disobedience." Chicago: Kerr, 1989.

Thoreau, Henry David. *Civil Disobedience and Other Essays.* Courier Dover Publications, 1993.

Thoreau, Henry David. *Walden, or, Life in the Woods.* New York: Dover, 1995.

Warner, Terry. *Bonds That Make Us Free: Healing Our Relationships, Coming to Ourselves.* Ann Arbor: Arbinger, 2001.

Wethington, Elaine. "Turning Points as Opportunities for Psychological Growth." In Corey Keyes and Jonathan Haidt (eds.), *Flourishing: Positive Psychology and the Life Well Lived.* Washington, DC: American Psychological Association, 2003.

Youngblood, Mark. *Life at the Edge of Chaos: Creating the Quantum Organization.* Dallas: Perceval Press, 1997.

ABOUT THE AUTHOR

Robert E. Quinn holds the Margaret Elliot Tracey Collegiate Professorship at the University of Michigan and serves on the faculty of Organization and Management at the Ross Business School. He is one of the cofounders and the current director of the Center for Positive Organizational Scholarship. His research and teaching interests focus on leadership, organizational change, and effectiveness. He has published sixteen books on these subjects, including *Deep Change: Discovering the Leader Within; Change the World: How Ordinary People Can Accomplish Extraordinary Results; Building the Bridge As You Walk On It: A Guide for Leading Change;* and *Lift: Becoming a Positive Force in Any Situation.*

INDEX